A BIBLIOGRAPHIC

INTRODUCTION TO NATIONALISM

BY

KOPPEL S. PINSON

WITH A FOREWORD BY
CARLTON J. H. HAYES

NEW YORK: MORNINGSIDE HEIGHTS

COLUMBIA UNIVERSITY PRESS

M · CM · XXXV

FOREWORD

As a student of modern nationalism, I have been painfully aware both of the need and of the lack of a critical bibliographical guide to the subject. To prepare such a guide is, of course, a difficult and hazardous undertaking. No reflective person and certainly no student of contemporary politics, economics, or international relations can fail to be impressed by the all-pervasive character and influence of nationalist phenomena or to entertain some curiosity as to what nationalism essentially is and how and why it has become an all-important factor in present-day thought and action. Yet, despite the obvious importance and pervasiveness of the subject, much of the literary treatment of it has been superficial in nature and propagandist in purpose, engendering more heat than light, and unfortunately serving to obscure the fact that some really scholarly studies have latterly been made and published on various aspects of nationalism.

The more these scholarly studies have multiplied, however, the more desirable it has become to sort them out of the mass of ephemeral popular writing and to catalogue them. Five years ago, with the financial assistance of the Social Science Research Council and the able personal assistance of Dr. Shepard B. Clough, Instructor in History in Columbia College, I made a preliminary survey of European and American research then being carried on in the field. Now, Dr. Koppel S. Pinson, utilizing the materials collected in that survey and greatly extending and supplementing them from his own research as well as from his experience as Assistant Editor of the Encyclopaedia of the Social Sciences, presents the following annotated list of general treatises and special monographs as an introductory bibliographical guide to the serious study of nationalism.

Dr. Pinson is not less aware than I of the provisional and tentative character of this bibliography. It is the first of its kind. It is frankly experimental. It has perfectly obvious limitations. For myself and for my own students, nevertheless, I am profoundly grateful to Dr. Pinson for preparing an original and truly serviceable guide and to the Columbia University Press for publishing it, and I believe that others will be similarly grateful.

New York   CARLTON J. H. HAYES,

April 15, 1935   PROFESSOR OF HISTORY IN COLUMBIA UNIVERSITY

PREFACE

The subject of nationalism is so broad in its scope, penetrates so deeply into all aspects of social, political, cultural and economic life, and is so amenable to purely propagandist purposes that the matter of selection in a bibliography of this kind is both delicate and difficult. Certain guiding principles for inclusion and exclusion have been adopted. Since this guide is intended primarily for the American student and reader it was considered advisable to include only works published in the English, French and German languages. Works published in other languages are included only if found in English, French or German translation.

A difficult problem in the selection of titles resulted from the very wide ramifications of the subject of nationalism. It is impossible to study any specific aspect of nationalism without going into the broader political, economic and cultural backgrounds of the particular age, country or individual. To include general works of such a nature, however, would so extend the limits of this work as to make it a bibliography of universal history rather than of nationalism. There are, it is true, many large general works on history, literature, philosophy, etc., not included here, which the student will find indispensable for his own investigations. It was considered wiser, however, to limit this bibliography to works which, either in whole or in part, deal specifically with the problems of nationalism.

Another group of works which has been omitted is comprised of books dealing with the purely juristic, administrative and formal political aspects of the nationality problem. There is a voluminous literature of such a character particularly with reference to the minorities problem. The reader is referred to Jacob Robinson's bibliographical guide to the minorities problem (see No. 56) and to the periodical, *Nation und Staat*, published in Vienna, for such references and accounts.

A more difficult problem in selection was raised by the older literature on nationalism. The beginnings of the study of nationalism are most intimately bound up with the very growth of the national movements themselves. The earliest works on nationalism were, for the most part, by inspirers, theorists and political leaders of the national movements in the various countries of western Europe, who published their works as part of the national struggle. All such works are now more important as influences within the historical development of nationalism than as scientific and objective studies of the subject itself. They may, perhaps, be termed the source materials for the study of nationalism. Only a few of the earlier works, like those of John Stuart Mill, Ernest Renan, J. K. Bluntschli and Francis Lieber, still retain their value as more or less objective treatments. In place of the large number of older works, therefore, the section on each geographical region has been prefaced by a list of writers whose works are of leading importance in the development of the nationalism and national spirit in their respective countries. In the case of most of these writers, moreover, it is the collected literary activity of the individual which is to be studied rather than any specific works. There is no single work of Herder, Schlegel, Chateaubriand or Barrès, for example, which may be pointed to as representing their specific contribution to the development of nationalism. The spirit of nationalism permeates all their work, whether it be on language, religion, politics, race, etc. For this reason, therefore, only the names of these writers have been listed, not the titles of their works.

Purely propagandist works, such as were produced during the World War, have also been excluded except where the material contained is valuable in itself or is not easily available elsewhere. In the case of periodical articles, only the most important have been included and, wherever possible, these have been related to books on the same subject.

The author feels indebted to very many individuals for making this work possible. He would hardly have felt competent to undertake such a task without the large store of material which he accumulated during his six years experience as Assistant Editor of the *Encyclopaedia of the Social Sciences*. He feels thankful, therefore, to the countless contributors and consultants of the *Encyclpaedia* as well as to the stimulating intellectual influence of his fellow editors. The author cannot refrain, however, from making special mention of a few people to whom he is particularly indebted. Professor Carlton Hayes of Columbia University has been generous with his advice and assistance throughout the entire period of the preparation of this work and I am profoundly grateful to him. I must also express my deep appreciation to Professor Hans Kohn of Smith College for many valuable suggestions as to method and content, to Dr. Gaudence Megaro of the College of the City of New York for helping me to gain a clearer conception of the problems of Italian nationalism, to Dr. Elsie Glück of the Women's Trade Union League for helpful advice on the section on Jewish nationalism and to Mr. Donald Porter Geddes of the Columbia University Press to whom more than to any other is due the practical realization of this project.

It is the intention of both the publishers and the author of this bibliographical guide to issue a revised and supplementary edition approximately every five years. The author, therefore, would gladly welcome communications from students and authors concerned with the problem of nationalism regarding their publications.

New York
April 1, 1935

KOPPEL S. PINSON

CONTENTS

THEORETICAL AND ANALYTICAL STUDIES (1–123) 1
General Analytical Works (1–56)
Psychological Studies (57–66)
Nationalism and Race (67–73)
Nationalism and Religion (74–78)
Nationalism and Language (79–82)
Nationalism and Politics (83–93)
Nationalism and Economic Affairs (94–104)
Nationalism, Socialism and Communism (105–10a)
Nationalism, Education and Propaganda (111–15)
National Minorities and National Autonomy (116–23)

HISTORICAL AND REGIONAL STUDIES (124–431) 19
NATIONALISM IN THE ANCIENT AND MEDIEVAL WORLDS (124–29) . . . 19
MODERN NATIONALISM IN THE WEST (130–377) 20
General Historical Surveys (130–41)
Nationalism in Germany and Austria (142–261a)
The Nationality Problem in the Austro-Hungarian Empire (217–26)
Nationalism in the Slavic World (227–54)
Nationalism in France (255–98)
Nationalism in Belgium and the Netherlands (299–306)
Nationalism in the Scandinavian Countries (307–13)
Nationalism in Switzerland (314–16)
Nationalism in Italy (317–44)
Nationalism in Spain, Portugal and Latin America (345–46)
Nationalism in Great Britain and the Dominions (347–66)
Nationalism in the United States (367–77a)

NATIONALISM IN THE ORIENT (378–409) 55
General Studies on the Orient (378–81)
Nationalism in the Near East (382–92)
Nationalism in the Far East (393–400)
Nationalism in India (401–9)

NATIONALISM AMONG THE JEWS (410–31) 59

INDEX OF NAMES 63

THEORETICAL AND ANALYTICAL STUDIES

GENERAL ANALYTICAL WORKS

See also Nos. 105, 106, 117a, 120, 233, 410, 421

1. HAYES, CARLTON JOSEPH HUNTLEY, *Essays on Nationalism* (New York, 1926), Macmillan, 279 pp.
This study is the most fundamental general analysis of the subject of nationalism. It is in large part responsible for the beginnings of the scientific investigation of the subject of nationalism in the United States. The author analyzes the theoretical bases of the concept, treats in broad outline of the rise and spread of nationalism, how it was propagated by groups of intellectuals among the broad masses, its similarities to a religious faith and its influence on international war, militarism and intolerance. See also the author's "Two Varieties of Nationalism: Original and Derived," in Association of History Teachers of the Middle States and Maryland, *Proceedings* (1928) No. XXVI, pp. 71-83.

2. GARNER, J. W., *Political Science and Government* (New York, 1928), American Book Co., x, 821 pp.
Chapters VI and VII, pp. 109-54, of this textbook in political science contain an admirable brief introduction to the problems of nationality, nation state and national minorities.

3. BUELL, RAYMOND LESLIE, *International Relations*, 2d ed. (New York, 1929), Henry Holt and Co., xix, 838 pp.
This work contains a cursory discussion of the "Sentiment of Nationality" in Ch. I; of the various pan-movements in Ch. IV; of economic nationalism in Ch. V, and of minorities in Ch. VIII.

4. JOHANNET, RÉNÉ, *Le Principe des nationalités*, 2d ed. (Paris, 1923), Nouvelle Librairie Nationale, 454 pp.
This is a thorough study of nationalism by an opponent of the nationalist principle and one who sees in it a source of great danger. The work contains an historical account of the use and development of the terminology; a very detailed exposition of the historical development of French nationalism from earliest times; the contrast between the ethnic basis of German theories of nationalism and the French theories based on subjective choice, and the political and international aspects of the nationality problem.

5. MITSCHERLICH, WALDEMAR, *Nationalismus: Die Geschichte einer Idee* (Leipzig, 1929), L. C. Hirschfeld, xi, 373 pp.
This is a new but practically unchanged edition of *Der Nationalismus Westeuropas*, which appeared in 1920. It represents a genetic approach to the problem. The author distinguishes three social stages: (1) social life with unconsciousness of individuality of either the individual or of the social groups, which is the prenationalist stage; (2) social life with consciousness of individuality in the individual but not in social groups, which represents the period of early nationalism; (3) social life with consciousness of individuality of both persons and groups, which is the nationalist epoch. He attributes the rise of nationalism in modern times

to (1) the growth of political centralization, (2) the unification of economic life, (3) the development of a general culture.
Cf. No. 10.

6. MITSCHERLICH, W., "Volk und Nation," in *Handwörterbuch der Soziologie*, ed. by Alfred Vierkandt (Stuttgart, 1931), Ferdinand Enke Verlag, pp. 644–52.
This presents a good summary of No. 5.

7. BOEHM, MAX HILDEBERT, *Das eigenständige Volk: Volkstheoretische Grundlagen der Ethnopolitik und Geisteswissenschaften* (Göttingen, 1932), Bandenhoeck und Ruprecht, 389 pp.
This is a very ambitious attempt at establishing a "science of nationalism." The author goes into the most minute analysis of the various aspects of the problem of nationalism, a process which often results in the overelaboration of very obvious facts and propositions. He takes a strongly national and conservative antidemocratic position; he attributes the evils of modern political nationalism to the French Revolution and the spread of democracy, distinguishes sharply between the German idea of nationalism and that of Western Europe, and is most vitally interested in the problem of national minorities. In this connection he develops the interesting idea of conationalism which is to serve to unite the members of a given nationality who are divided among more than one political state. An excellent English summary of this author's views is found in his article on the theoretical aspects of nationalism in the *Encyclopaedia of the Social Sciences*, XI (1933), pp. 231–40.

8. JOSEPH, BERNARD, *Nationality, Its Nature and Problems* (New Haven, 1929), Yale University Press, 380 pp.
The author, an ardent Jewish nationalist, proceeds from the conviction "that the only satisfactory and enduring basis of society is the complete recognition of the principle of nationality." The first part is a theoretical discussion of the factors of nationality and the second half deals with historical developments in Europe, the British Empire and India, and among the national groups of the East, the Jews and the Americans. The work in attempting too much is, as a result, very superficial in many places and repeats many "nationalistic errors" rejected by most scientific writers.

9. ZIEGLER, HEINZ O., *Die moderne Nation: ein Beitrag zur politischen Soziologie* (Tübingen, 1931), J. C. B. Mohr, viii, 308 pp.
This is a sociological and philosophical analysis of contemporary nationalism with monographic studies on the contributions to nationalist theory of Hegel, Ranke, Stahl, Lorenz von Stein, Gneist, Treitschke, and Constantin Frantz. The author regards the nation as the "concept which provides the sanction of legitimacy to the modern state." He considers nationalism a purely modern manifestation brought about largely by the French Revolution and the democratic idea. He draws a sharp distinction between the German idea of a *Kulturnation* and the nationalism of the Western-European nations.

10. FELS, JOSEF, *Begriff und Wesen der Nation: eine soziologische Untersuchung und Kritik* (Münster, 1927), Aschendorff, xv, 147 pp. "Deutschtum und Aussland," Heft VI.
This is an extremely useful work for the clarification of the terms and concepts used in the literature on nationalism. The author analyzes in detail in this connection the views of Franz Oppenheimer, Otto Bauer, Alfred Vierkandt, Ignaz Seipel, Friedrich Meinecke, and Waldemar Mitscherlich and then applies the same sort of analysis to the various distinguishing marks set up as tests of nationality—race, language, territory, religion, state, common culture and common will. The author's

own stand is that nationalism is a historical process which must be sub-
ordinated to a higher unity.

11. JERUSALEM, FRANZ W., *Über den Begriff der Nation* (Jena, 1932),
G. Fischer, 28 pp.
The author holds that the nation is a product of the collective urge and
its origin is therefore due not to common language, religion or history, but
rather to a common political organization under the absolutist state.

12. KIRCHHOFF, ALFRED, *Zur Verständigung über die Begriffe Nation und
Nationalität* (Halle a. S., 1905), Buchhandlung des Waisenhauses,
64 pp.
The author distinguishes between the ethnic concept *Volk*, and the political
concept, *Staat*. The first represents the *Kulturnation*, the second the
Staatsnation.
Cf. Stavenhagen, Kurt, "Das Problem Kulturnation und der Staats-
nation," in *Nation und Staat*, V (1932), 666-718.

13. ROSENBLUTH, FELIX, *Zur Begriffsbestimmung von Volk und Nation* (Berlin, 1910), Emil Ebering, 45 pp.
An analysis of the use of the terms, nation, people, national character,
national consciousness, etc., in the older literature of nationalism.

14. BOHN, ANDRÉ, *Essai sur la notion de nationalité dans le principe des
nationalités* (Nancy, 1923), Imprimerie Nancéenne, 97 pp.
A formalistic doctoral dissertation concerned chiefly with the problem
of definition of terms.

15. RENAN, ERNEST, *Qu'est-ce qu'une nation?* (Paris, 1882), C. Lévy, 30 pp.,
reprinted in his *Discours et conférences* (Paris, 1887), C. Lévy, pp.
277-310.
The classic French definition of nationality as based on a common cultural heritage and a common desire to persist as a nationality.

16. BARTH, PAUL, *Die Philosophie der Geschichte als Soziologie*, 3d and 4th
eds. (Leipzig, 1922), O. R. Reisland.
In pages 797-824 the author analyzes the idea of nationality as a leading
concept of the philosophy of history. He believes that nationality is
neither the first stage nor the final goal of society. It has its roots in
other ideas and is only an intermediate stage to higher unities. Therefore
this concept cannot be taken as a fundamental one in historical development. He traces the idea of nationality in sociological and anthropological terms from the original feeling of kinship, through the corporate
feeling of belonging to a state developed among the Greeks, the widening
of the concept to include humanity in the Hellenistic period, its various
ups and downs in the Middle Ages and early modern times up to the
national struggle for power in the nineteenth century.

17. SEIPEL, IGNAZ, *Nation und Staat* (Vienna, 1916), Wilhelm Braumüller,
xx, 195 pp.
A very penetrating and philosophical analysis, by a leading Austrian
Catholic, of nationalism and religion, of the relation of nationalities to
each other in a multinational state and of international relations. Written during the World War, it shows the influence of the war spirit and
of the peculiar nationality problem in Austria-Hungary.
Cf. No. 10.

18. SCHELER, MAX, *Nation und Weltanschauung*, Vol. II of his *Schriften zur
Soziologie und Weltanschauungslehre* (Leipzig, 1923), Der Neue Geist
Verlag, viii, 174 pp.
A collection of essays containing "Über die Nationalideen der grossen
Nationen," pp. 1-18; "Das Nationale im Denken Frankreichs," pp. 19-65;
Der Geist und die ideelen Grundlagen der Demokratien der grossen

Nationen," pp. 66–116. Scheler attacks the subjective and political ideas of nationality. He defines a nation as a cultural unity and holds that the clash of peoples is due to the great opposition between *Weltanschauungen*. In characterizing the missionary ideals of various nations, he maintains that German nationalism reveals the absence of this characteristic more than any other nationalism.

19. TAGORE, RABINDRANATH, *Nationalism* (New York, 1917), Macmillan, 159 pp.
Tagore discusses nationalism in the West, in Japan and in India. He presents a most appealing criticism of the concept of the national state as developed in the West.

20. ZANGWILL, ISRAEL, *The Principle of Nationalities* (New York, 1917), Macmillan, 111 pp.
Although no more than a pamphlet, it is a very keen analysis of the principle of nationality. Zangwill defines nationality as "a state of mind corresponding to a political fact."

21. BENDA, JULIEN, *The Treason of the Intellectuals*, translated from the French by Richard Aldington (New York, 1928), William Morrow, xii, 244 pp.
A scathing arraignment of modern nationalism and the part played in its development by intellectuals whose profession should have led them to extol the universal rather than the particular. The author's basic idea is that particularism itself is evil and leads to conflict and hatred. He throws light on many implications involved in the development of nationalism. The book is more interesting for its provocative character than for its intrinsic soundness.

22. BENDA, JULIEN, *La Fin de l'éternel* (Paris, 1929), Librairie Gallimard, 263 pp.
A reply to critics of the author's *Treason of the Intellectuals*. (See No. 21.)

23. BENDA, JULIEN, *Discours à la nation européenne* (Paris, 1933), Librairie Gallimard, 237 pp.
An attack on nationalism and national states as the creations of nineteenth-century "dynamism," irrationality and romantic heroism. It is a plea for a return to clarity and rationalism and for the reconstruction of a new ideal of Europe (to take the place of the national ideals) based on the Gallo-Roman cultural traditions.

24. SPANN, OTHMAR, *Vom Wesen des Volkstums; Was ist deutsch*, 3d ed. (Berlin, 1929), Widerstands-Verlag, 62 pp.
The nation is a *Kulturgemeinschaft* based on common philosophy, morals, art and science. But the concept is a graded one. Thus only the few who are fully and thoroughly acquainted with German culture are the "real nation," while the rest may be only 80 percent, 60 percent, 20 percent German, etc.
The same ideas are developed systematically in the author's *Gesellschaftslehre*, 3d ed. (Leipzig, 1930), Quelle und Meyer, pp. 457–82.

25. BARKER, ERNEST, *National Character and the Factors in Its Formation* (London, 1927), Harper and Bros., vi, 288 pp.
The author defines a nation as a material basis (consisting of race, territory and economic conditions) with a spiritual superstructure (law and government, religion, language and literature, education). National character is "the sum of acquired tendencies which a national society has built on the native basis of its racial blend, its territory and the mass and social variety of its population." The book is an analysis of each of these factors with special attention to the growth and development of English national character. There is a good deal of emphasis on the

political aspects of nationalism with the belief that territory and political unity are the essential physical bases of nationality. The national character of the English, he concludes, consists of (1) energy, (2) initiative, (3) individual responsibility before God in religion, (4) economic doctrine of voluntary enterprise, (5) liberty.

Cf. HERTZ, FRIEDRICH, "Die Allgemeinen Theorien vom Nationalcharakter," in *Archiv für Sozialwissenschaft und Sozialpolitik*, LIV (1925) 1–35, 657–715.

26. PETRESCU, NICHOLAS, *The Interpretation of National Differentiations* (London, 1929), Watts and Co., vi, 293 pp.

National differentiations, the author holds, possess no permanent and essential forms of expression of social reality. They are like other actual or possible differentiations, only the temporary and gradual forms under which the social process manifests itself in time and place. They do not represent absolute values and have no meaning and no function except in relation to the social conditions and conceptions of a certain environment and under a certain stage of evolution. They are the effect and not the cause of the actual organization of civilized society.

27. MICHELS, ROBERTO, *Der Patriotismus: Prolegomena zu seiner soziologischen Analyse* (Munich, 1929), Dunker und Humblot, viii, 271 pp.

This is an attempt at a psychological analysis of the fatherland myth and national pride, of the feeling of love of home land, of the antipathy to foreigners, and of national folk songs and music. The book reveals a wide reading and acquaintance with the literature, but there is no integrated general conception of nationalism.

28. HERBERT, SYDNEY, *Nationality and Its Problems* (London, 1920), Methuen, ix, 173 pp.

The author bases nationality on geography, government, culture and religion. Political nationalism must yield before cultural nationalism and the national state before a multinational state.

29. VAN GENNEP, ARNOLD, *Traité comparatif des nationalités*, Vol. I, *Les Elements extérieures de la nationalité* (Paris, 1922), Payot, 228 pp.

This is the first of a projected three-volume work on nationality. The author, rejecting the subjective factors of nationality, attempts to study the physical, ethnological, linguistic and demographic aspects of nationality. In this volume, which is all that has appeared to date, he is concerned chiefly with national symbols.

30. LE FUR, LOUIS, *Races, Nationalités, États* (Paris, 1922), Félix Alcan, viii, 156 pp.

Neither race nor nationality, holds the author, is the uniting bond of social groups. The state represents the synthesis of all common factors such as language, territory, religion, etc., and it keeps the group together. The author condemns theories of nationality as inexact and dangerous.

31. BOAS, FRANZ, *Anthropology and Modern Life*, 2d ed. (New York, 1932), W. W. Norton, 255 pp.

Chapter IV, pp. 81–105, on "Nationalism," is a plea for national idealism and purely cultural nationalism as against racial and aggressive nationalism.

32. BRUNHES, JEAN, and CAMILLE VALLAUX, *La Géographie de l'histoire* (Paris, 1921), Félix Alcan.

The geographic aspects of the problem of nationalism are discussed on pp. 597–668.

33. ZIMMERN, ALFRED E., *Nationality and Government and Other War Time Essays* (London, 1918), Chatto and Windus, xxiv, 364 pp.

This contains several war-time essays (pp. 32–100) on problems of nationalism. The author affirms a positive attitude toward the principle of nationality, but emphasizes its subjective and cultural character as opposed to the objective character of the political state.

34. KRONENBERG, H., *Der politische Gedanke*, 4 vols. (Berlin, 1922–27), Deutsche Verlagsgesellschaft für Politik und Geschichte.
In Vol. I, *Der Menschheitsgedanke*, 79 pp., and Vol. II, *Der nationale Gedanke*, 72 pp., the author, a leading pacifist philosopher, attempts a synthesis of nationalism and internationalism which he hopes will do away with war.

35. STOCKS, J. L., *Patriotism and the Super State* (London, 1920), Swarthmore Press, 106 pp.
The author discusses the relation of the sentiment of patriotism to the state, the nation, and an international society of nations. He rejects the proposal to dispense with nationalism and presents a good psychological analysis of the patriotic sentiment.

36. VEBLEN, THORSTEIN, *An Inquiry into the Nature of Peace and the Terms of Its Perpetuation* (New York, 1917), Macmillan, xiii, 367 pp.
Chapters I–II, pp. 1–76, present a cosmopolitan and rationalistic analysis of patriotism and of such concepts as "national honor" and "national culture."

37. MUIR, RAMSAY, *Nationalism and Internationalism, the Culmination of Modern History* (London, 1917), Constable, 229 pp.
This is a brilliant and very popular survey of the history of modern national movements and of the growth of international thought and organization. It reflects the view held by liberals during the World War that the war was a step toward the triumph of liberty and justice.

38. HUNTER, EARLE LESLIE, *A Sociological Analysis of Certain Types of Patriotism. A Study of Certain Patriotic Attitudes, Particularly as They Appear in Peace-time Controversies in the United States* (New York, 1932), Paul Maisel Co., 263 pp.
After a study of six types of patriotism (state supremacy, institutional loyalty, national egocentrism, eclectic institutional loyalty, critical-mindedness toward the state and national self-sufficiency) the author concludes that loyalties are attached to specific ends and that patriotic loyalties are directed only to specific aspects of country. Wider national patriotism is only a sentimentalized and fictitious notion of country.

39. REIDENBACH, C., *A Critical Analysis of Patriotism as an Ethical Concept* (Indianapolis, 1922), Privately Printed, 127 pp.
This is a study of the impulses of patriotism, its habituation, its beliefs in country and its conflicts with internationalism. The study is lacking in originality and makes too extensive use of quotations.

40. PAGE, KIRBY, *National Defense: a Study of the Origins, Results and Prevention of War* (New York, 1931), Farrar and Rinehart, x, 403 pp.
A popular pacifistic denunciation of the relations to war of nationalism, imperialism, chauvinism and militarism.

41. KREHBIEL, EDWARD BENJAMIN, *Nationalism, War and Society* (New York, 1916), Macmillan, 176 pp.
A pacifistic outline of the fallacies of nationalism and national rivalries, presented in a very lucid and diagrammatic form, useful for class-room study.

42. PERLA, LEO, *What Is National Honor? The Challenge of the Reconstruction* (New York, 1918), Macmillan, xxx, 211 pp.
The practical suggestions of the book may now be disregarded. Its value lies in the brilliant exposé of how the concept of "national honor" has been used as an idealistic dressing for tangible material interests. It has a valuable series of quotations illustrating this point.

43. STEINMETZ, SEBALD RUDOLF, *Die Nationalitäten in Europa*, issued as supplement No. 2 to the *Zeitschrift der Gesellschaft für Erdkunde zu Berlin* (1927), 67 pp.
A survey of the nationalities in Europe with a general introduction to the problem. This is a summary of the author's larger work, published in Dutch, *De Nationaliteiten in Europa* (1920).

44. ANIN, MAXIM, *Die Nationalitätenprobleme der Gegenwart: eine staatsrechtliche-politische Studie* (Riga, 1910), Schnakenburg, 103 pp.
The author analyzes the nationality problem in Switzerland, Austria-Hungary, Russia, Turkey, and among the Jews.

45. TECHET, CARL, *Völker, Vaterländer, und Fürsten. Ein Beitrag zur Entwicklung Europas* (Munich, 1913), Lothar Joachim, x, 480 pp.
A plea for a European internationalism against the "Asiatic peril" and an analysis of the racial composition of European nationalities showing their wide mixture and diffusion.

46. WEINREICH, ECKART, *Die Nation als Lebensgemeinschaft*, (Munich, 1931), J. F. Lehman, 121 pp.
The acknowledgments to Paul Ernst, Leopold Ziegler and Nicholas Berdayev are sufficient to indicate the religious-mystical, conservative and antidemocratic tendencies of the author. After analyzing and rejecting the solutions offered by Socialism, Fascism and Bolshevism, he calls upon the German nation to infuse a new regenerating religious spirit of group feeling into the world.

47. BLAGOYÉVITCH, VEDAN, *Le Principe des nationalités et son application dans les traités de paix de Versailles et de Saint Germain* (Paris, 1922), Éditions de "la Vie Universitaire," 457 pp.
A thoroughly eclectic work. Together with a narrative account of the attention given by the World War treaties to the various national "sore spots" there is an account of the development of French nationalism and a theoretical section dealing with the concepts of nation and national factors, which is mainly interesting for its classification and listing of the different types of definitions.

48. BLUNTSCHLI, JOHANN KASPAR, *Gesammelte kleine Schriften*, 2 vols. (Nördlingen, 1879–81), C. H. Beckschen Buchhandlung, 319 and 313 pp.
Three essays in this collection are important for the problem of nationalism:
(1) "Die nationale Staatenbildung und der moderne deutsche Staat," pp. 70–113, which deals with general definitions of nationality and its relations to the formation of political national states;
(2) "Die schweizerische Nationalität," pp. 114–31, which affirms the existence of a distinct Swiss nationality but not on the basis of race, language or common interests but rather as the creation of political ideas.
(3) "Einwirkung der Nationalität auf die Religion und kirchliche Dinge," pp. 132–47.

49. *Verhandlungen des zweiten deutschen Soziologentages*, Schriften der Deutschen Gesellschaft für Soziologie, First Series, Vol. II, (Tübingen, 1913), J. C. B. Mohr, 192 pp.
Contains: (1) BARTH, PAUL, "Die Nationalität in ihrer soziologischer Bedeutung," pp. 21–48; (2) SCHMID, FERDINAND, "Das Recht der Nationalitäten," pp. 55–71, which is a discussion of the constitutional problems involved in the nationality problem; (3) HARTMANN, LUDO MORITZ, "Die Nation als politischer Faktor," pp. 80–97, which is an attack on the views of Renner and Otto Bauer and which suggests the possibility of peaceful assimilation of nationalities; (4) OPPENHEIMER, FRANZ, "Die rassentheoretische Geschichtsphilosophie," pp. 98–139; (5) MICHELS, ROBERT,

"Die historische Entwicklung des Vaterlandsgedankens," pp. 140–84; and discussions of these papers by Ferdinand Tönnies, Max Weber, Eduard Bernstein, Alfred Weber, Heinrich Driesmanns and others.

50. SALOMON, G., editor, *Nation und Nationalität*, Supplement to *Jahrbuch fur Soziologie* (Karlsruhe, 1927), G. Braun, x, 217 pp.
Contains: (1) HERTZ, FRIEDRICH, "Wesen und Werden der Nation," pp. 1–88, a very comprehensive survey of the use of the concept of nationality since ancient times;
(2) STEINMETZ, SEBALD RUDOLF, "Die Nationalität und ihr Wille," pp. 89–115, which presents the characteristics of nationality and an appraisal of the value of nationalism;
(3) BOEHM, MAX HILDEBERT, "Die Nationalitätenfrage," pp. 116–51, which deals chiefly with the political aspects of the national question, their relation to the postwar treaties and the idea of national autonomy;
(4) ROFFENSTEIN, GASTON, "Zur Soziologie des Nationalismus und der nationale Parteien," pp. 152–99, which is a sociological analysis of the attitudes and social tendencies engendered by nationalism, with special attention to Marxism, militarism and intellectualism;
(5) KÁRMÁN, ELMER VON, "Psychologie der Internationalismus," pp. 207–17, which considers the international factors counteracting nationalist tendencies.

51. ARISTOTELIAN SOCIETY, *Proceedings* (London, 1920) n. s. XX, 237–65.
Very brief attempts at definitions of nationality and nationalism by ÉLIE HALÉVY, MARCEL MAUSS, THEODORE RUYSSEN, RENÉ JOHANNET, GILBERT MURRAY and SIR FREDERICK POLLOCK.

52. *Ethnopolitischer Almanach. Ein Führer durch die europäische National- itäten Bewegung*, edited by Otto Junghann and Max Hildebert Boehm (Vienna, 1930), Wilhelm Braumüller, viii, 182 pp.
Volume I contains a series of articles on various aspects of nationalism and minorities. Among others are: (1) BROECKER, RUDOLPH, "Völkerrecht- Minderheitenrecht-Volksrecht," pp. 1–9; (2) HASSELBLATT, WERNER, "Kul- turautonomie," pp. 10–19; (3) ROBINSON, JACOB, "Der altjüdische Auto- nomie Begriff," pp. 20–24; (4) RASCHHOFER, HERMAN, "Die nationale Kurie," pp. 25–36; (5) CIHLAR, SLAVKO, "Der Zusammenbruch des Jugo- slavimus," pp. 37–48; (6) BERNDT, FEDERLEY, "Nationalitätenfragen in Finnland," pp. 49–60; (7) BOEHM, M. H., "Zur Geschichte der internatio- nalitären Bewegung," pp. 61–71.

53. LOESCH, K. C. VON, and A. H. ZIEGFELD, editors, *Volk unter Völkern*, (Breslau, 1925), Ferdinand Hirt, 453 pp. "Bücher des Deutschtums" of the Deutscher Schutzbund, Vol. 1.
Contains among others:
(1) BOEHM, M. H., "Staatsgewalt und Nationalitätenproblem," pp. 192– 208, in which the author points to the inadequacy of the form of the demo- cratic state of Western Europe to cope with the nationality problem in Central and Eastern Europe; (2) VRIES, AXEL DE, "Die Nationalitäten- politik Sowjetrusslands und die Fehler der Westeuropäischen Staaten," pp. 377–82; (3) HINTZE, HEDWIG, "Der französische Regionalismus," pp. 349–76.

54. LOESCH, KARL C. VON, editor, *Staat und Volkstum* (Berlin, 1926), Deut- scher Schutzbund Verlag, 799 pp. "Bücher des Deutschtums" of the Deutscher Schutzbund, Vol. II.
Contains among others:
(1) LOESCH, K. C. VON, "Paneuropa-Völker und Staaten," pp. 7–50; (2) TONNESSEN, JOHANNES, "Volkstum und nationale Gedanke," pp. 116–27; (3) ULLMANN, HERMANN, "Antriebe und Quellen der Anschluss-

bewegung, pp. 128–44; (4) HUGELMANN, KARL, "Die Anschlussbewegung in Oesterreich," pp. 145–54; (5) HASSELBLATT, WERNER, "Die Durchführung der Kulturautonomie in Estland," pp. 155–63; (6) FIRCKS, WILHELM, "Minderheitenautonomie in Lettland," pp. 164–71; (7) ERNST, ROBERT, "Der Autonomiegedanke in Elsass-Lothringen," pp. 172–79; (8) JAKABSSY, ELEMER, "Die ungarische Minoritäten und der europäische Minderheitengedanke," pp. 180–87; (9) OUDENDIJK, K. E., "Die grossniederländische Bewegung," pp. 260–66; (10) D'ARTOIS, J., "Die nationale Entwicklung der Wallonen," pp. 267–78.

55. BARNES, HARRY ELMER, *History and Social Intelligence* (New York, 1926), A. Knopf, xvii, 597 pp.
Chapter IV, "The Historical Development of Nationalism," pp. 145–92, is a reprint of the author's article in the *Encyclopaedia Americana,* and Ch. V, pp. 193–217, deals with "Nationalism and Historical Writing."

56. ROBINSON, JACOB, *Das Minoritäten Problem und seine Literatur* (Berlin, 1928), Walter de Gruyter und Co., 265 pp. Institut für ausländisches öffentliches Recht und Völkerrecht, "Beiträge," Heft. VI.
A bibliography chiefly devoted to the minorities problem. Its usefulness is marred considerably by its poor arrangement.
Important general analytical articles on nationalism are: HANDMAN, MAX S., "The Sentiment of Nationalism," in *Political Science Quarterly,* XXVI, (1921), 104–21; SULZBACH, WALTER, "Begriff und Wesen der Nation," in *Die Dioskuren,* II (1923), 128–59; BUBNOFF, NICOLAI VON, "Der Begriff der Nation und die Idee einer Völkergemeinschaft," in *Archiv für Sozialwissenschaft und Sozialpolitik,* LI (1923), 110–68; EISENMANN, LOUIS, "Quelques aspects nouveaux de l'idée de nationalité," in the International Committee of Historical Sciences, *Bulletin,* II (1929), 225–33.

PSYCHOLOGICAL STUDIES

See also Nos. 27, 35, 121, 350, 366

57. MILLER, HERBERT ADOLPHUS, *Races, Nations and Classes. The Psychology of Domination and Freedom* (Philadelphia, 1924), J. B. Lippincott Co., xvii, 196 pp. "The Lippincott Sociological Series."
The author's thesis is that only the application of psychological laws to social relations to foster harmony between two groups can secure international peace. The problems discussed include national conflicts in Central Europe, Ireland, French Canada, India, Mexico and Korea; religion and anti-Semitism; linguistic problems and attempts at Americanization. A solution is possible only through plural sovereignty and a recognition that national loyalty is neither the only nor the supreme loyalty.

58. PARTRIDGE, G. E., *The Psychology of Nations. A Contribution to the Philosophy of History* (New York, 1919), Macmillan, xii, 333 pp.
The first part is a psychological analysis of the effects of national consciousness on wars. The second part deals with educational factors in the development of nations and is a plea for international-mindedness in education.

59. PILLSBURY, W. B., *The Psychology of Nationality and Internationalism* (New York, 1919), D. Appleton and Co., x, 314 pp.
The author takes a compromise position between MacDougall's theory of immediate instinct and Trotter's idea of the dominance of convention and "herd instinct." He views nationality as a psychological and sociological problem shown largely in responses that betray a man's emotional

and intellectual activities. He studies the relative importance of the social instincts of sympathy and hate, and also the phenomenon of naturalization and change in nationality.

See also Allport, F. H. "The Psychology of Nationalism," in *Harper's Monthly*, CLV (1927), 291–301.

60. STRATTON, GEORGE MALCOMB, *Social Psychology of International Conduct* (New York, 1929), D. Appleton and Co., x, 387 pp.
A textbook of the international scene from the standpoint of psychology. He surveys the causes of racial prejudice, national desires and ways of developing an international mind.
Cf. also No. 50.

61. HOBSON, JOHN A., *The Psychology of Jingoism* (London, 1901), Grant Richards, 139 pp.
A study of nationalist propaganda through the church, press and lecture platform. This work was inspired by the Boer War.

62. LE BON, GUSTAVE, *The Psychology of Peoples*, translated from the French (London, 1899), T. Fisher Unwin, xx, 236 pp.
This work is by the leading exponent of the theory of "national character" or "soul of a race" as the explanation of history.
Cf. Barnes, H. E., "A Psychological Interpretation of Modern Social Problems and of Contemporary History: A Survey of the Contributions of Gustave Le Bon to Social Psychology," in *American Journal of Psychology*, XXXI (1920), 333–69.

63. FOUILLÉE, ALFRED, *Esquisse psychologique des peuples européennes*, 2d ed. (Paris, 1903), Félix Alcan, xix, 550 pp.
This is the most ambitious attempt at setting up a psychology of peoples. Fouillée believed that each people possesses a *vouloir-vivre collectif* which expresses itself in common tendencies, common sentiments and common ideas.
Cf. No. 70.

64. MCDOUGALL, WILLIAM, *The Group Mind. A Sketch of the Principles of Collective Psychology with Some Attempt to Apply Them to the Interpretation of National Life and Character*, 2d ed. (New York, 1920), G. P. Putnam's Sons, xxii, 418 pp.
Parts II and III, pps. 135–413, deal with an analysis of what constitutes national mind and character and their development. The author's theory, that of a Nordic racialist, is aristocratic, and is based on the idea of racial and biological selection.

65. MCDOUGALL, WILLIAM, *Ethics and Some Modern World Problems* (New York, 1924), G. P. Putnam's Sons, xvii, 256 pp.
The author takes a stand against universal ethics with its humanitarianism, democracy and socialism. He foresees the biological danger of overbreeding of inferior races and nations at the expense of the superior ones and asserts the principle of nationality and of aristocracy. This work is a sequel to No. 64.

66. MADARIAGA, SALVADOR DE, *Englishmen, Frenchmen, Spaniards; an Essay in Comparative Psychology*, (London, 1928), Oxford University Press, xix, 256 pp.
This is not an attempt at a scientific study. The author bases this study of national psychology only on "intuitional knowledge." He brilliantly characterizes the English as a people of action, the French as a nation of thinkers, and the Spaniards as a people of passion.

NATIONALISM AND RACE

See also Nos. 31, 49, 258, 260, 347, 414.

67. HERTZ, FRIEDRICH, *Race and Civilization*, translated from the German by A. S. Levetus and W. Entz (London, 1928), Macmillan, xii, 328 pp.
A scientific sociological and anthropological attack upon the theories of racial superiority, with a full discussion of the leading theories that have been advanced.

68. HANKINS, FRANK H., *The Racial Basis of Civilization. A Critique of the Nordic Doctrine* (New York, 1926), Alfred A. Knopf, xi, 384 pp.
The most dispassionate history and criticism of the various types of racial theories.

69. SIMAR, THÉOPHILE, *Étude critique sur la formation de la doctrine des races au xviiie siécle et son expansion au xixe siècle*, Académie royale de Belgique, Classe des Lettres et des Sciences morales et politiques, *Memoires*, Second Series, XVI (1922), No. 4, 403 pp.
A comprehensive discussion and critique of race theories in Europe and America, tying them up with nationalist philosophy.

70. FINOT, JEAN, *Race Prejudice*, translated from the French by Florence Wade-Evans (London, 1906), Archibald Constable and Co., xvi, 320 pp.
A damning attack on racialist theories. Part III is especially important for its critique of the science of psychology of peoples. The author deniés any stability to national character. He holds that it is too complex and too ever-changing to lend itself to clear analysis. He criticizes particularly the works of Fouillée, Renan, Taine, etc.

71. ENGELN, OSCAR DIEDRICH VON, *Inheriting the Earth; or the Geographical Factor in National Development* (New York, 1922), Macmillan, xvi, 379 pp.
A detailed consideration of physical environment as a factor in nationality and an attack on the theory that nationality is based essentially on race.

72. KEITH, ARTHUR, *Nationality and Race from an Anthropologist's Point of View*, (London, 1919), Oxford University Press, 39 pp.
The author presents the thesis that modern racial strife and national agitations reveal man's inherited tribal instincts at war with his present-day conditions of life.

73. PEARSON, KARL, *National Life from the Standpoint of Science*, 2d ed. (London, 1905), A. and C. Black, xi, 106 pp.
This is Darwinian racialist interpretation of nationalism, combined with an aggressive imperialism clothed in scientific concepts that have since been seriously questioned.

NATIONALISM AND RELIGION

See also Nos. 1, 17, 48, 57, 129, 144, 269, 270, 273, 280, 368, 388.

74. BARKER, ERNEST, *Christianity and Nationality* (Oxford, 1927), Clarendon Press, 32 pp.
A sane and moderate attempt to harmonize modern nationalism with the doctrines of Christianity and the problems of the church. This lecture is reprinted in the author's *Church, State and Study* (London, 1930), Methuen, pp. 131–50.
Cf. also Lenz, Max, "Nationalität und Religion," in *Preussische Jahrbücher*, CXXVII. (1907), 385–408.

75. GRENTRUP, THEODORE, *Religion und Muttersprache* (Münster, 1932), Aschendorff, viii, 550 pp. "Deutschtum und Ausland," Heft XLVII–XLIX.

The author, a Catholic writer, gives a scientific exposition of the attitude of religion toward the secular aspects of a national language, and the use of the national language in the sphere of religion. He treats of both Catholic and Protestant faiths.

76. CECIL, LORD HUGH RICHARD HEATHCOTE, *Nationalism and Catholicism* (London, 1919), Macmillan, 64 pp.

A plea that the universal church act as a moderating influence on excessive nationalism.

77. VAUSSARD, MAURICE, editor, *Enquête sur le nationalisme* (Paris, 1924), Éditions Spes, 413 pp.

The question "How can nationalism be harmonized with the universality of the Catholic church?" is answered by leading Catholics: theologians and philosophers such as Batiffol, Maurice Blondel and Jacques Chevalier; social scientists like Louis Le Fur and Paul Bureau; writers like Georges Goyau, Ernest Seilliére, René Pinon, René Johannet, Hillaire Belloc, John Ryan, Count Apponyi, Luigi Sturzo and O. Halecki.

78. SCHLUND, ERHARD, *Katholizismus und Vaterland*, 3d ed. (Munich, 1925), F. A. Pfeiffer, 96 pp.

This is an attempt to harmonize national patriotism with Catholic theology. The work also contains some Catholic exceptions to the national doctrine of Fascism and National Socialism.

Cf. also Mausbach, J., "Nationalismus und christlicher Universalismus," in *Hochland*, IX (1912).

NATIONALISM AND LANGUAGE

See also Nos. 75, 96, 261, 427, 428.

79. DOMINIAN, LEON, *The Frontiers of Language and Nationality in Europe* (New York, 1917), Henry Holt, xviii, 375 pp.

This is mainly a factual account of the extent and use of the various national languages in Europe, emphasizing the geographical influences at work in the formation of nationality.

80. VOSSLER, KARL, *The Spirit of Language in Civilization*, translated from the German by Oscar Oeser (London, 1932), Kegan Paul, Trench, Trubner and Co., vii, 247 pp.

Chapter VII, pp. 107–74, deals with language as a national problem. Cf. also Buck, Carl Darling, "Language and the Sentiment of Nationality," in *American Political Science Review*, X (1916), 44–69; and Stavenhagen, Kurt, "Volk und Muttersprache," in *Nation und Staat*, III (1930), 491–524, 584–98.

81. SCHMIDT-ROHR, GEORG, *Die Sprache als Bildnerin der Völker. Eine Wesens– und Lebenskunde der Volkstümer* (Jena, 1932), Eugen Diederichs Verlag, 418 pp.

This is a most detailed, but somewhat ponderous, exposition of language as the basis of nationalism. The author distinguishes between *Volk*, which he calls a *Wesensgemeinschaft*, and *Nation*, which is a *Willensgemeinschaft*. The second part of the book is devoted chiefly to the situation in Germany and to a call for Germany to assert itself as a *Nation*. He attacks Nordic racialism and anti-Semitism as the two leading factors which stand in the way of this national realization. The second edition of this work, published under the title *Mutter Sprache* (Jena, 1933), 457 pp., has been revised to fit in more readily with the principles of National Socialism now dominant in Germany.

82. AUCAMP, ANNA JACOBA, *Bilingual Education and Nationalism with Special Reference to South Africa* (Pretoria, 1926), J. L. Van Schaik, 247 pp.
A statistical treatment of the important question of bilingualism, mainly from a pedagogic standpoint. It lacks an adequate conceptual approach but is useful for the material collected on bilingualism in Wales, Scotland, Ireland, Canada, Belgium and South Africa, as well as for some valuable historical material.

NATIONALISM AND POLITICS

83. MILL, JOHN STUART, *Considerations on Representative Government* (London, 1861), Parker and Brown, viii, 340 pp.
This work is important chiefly for historical reasons. Chapter XVI, "Of Nationality as Connected with Representative Government," is the plea of a liberal for the recognition of the principle of nationality and the identification of nationality with the nation state. Translated into the languages of subject nationalities, this work had a tremendous influence on the shaping of nationalist ideology.

84. LIEBER, FRANCIS, *Fragments of Political Science on Nationalism and Internationalism* (New York, 1868), Scribners, 23 pp.
This is the first important work on nationalism published in the United States. It is a beautiful illustration of German liberal nationalism transplanted to the United States, with an attempt to apply its principles to the American scene.

85. BLUNTSCHLI, JOHANN KASPAR, *The Theory of the State*, translated from the German by D. G. Ritchie, P. E. Matheson and R. Lodge (Oxford, 1892), Clarendon Press.
In pages 81–108 the author takes up the problem of nationality and its relation to the state. He recognizes the natural goal of every nationality to be a political state. This is one of the more important older works on nationality.

86. ACTON, LORD, "Nationality," in *The History of Freedom and Other Essays* (London, 1909), Macmillan, pp. 289-98.
A bitter attack on political nationalism. The uninational state is tyrannical, whereas "the State which is multinational may be limited and checked by the play and interplay of its contained nations." Acton was one of the few earlier liberal writers who saw the dangers of nationalism.

87. MERRIAM, CHARLES EDWARD, *The Making of Citizens, a Comparative Study of Methods of Civic Training* (Chicago, 1931), University of Chicago Press, xv, 371 pp.
One of the volumes in the series of "Studies in the Making of Citizens," edited by Charles E. Merriam. This volume by the editor of the series draws together the threads from all the other volumes and presents a summary of their conclusions. The emphasis in this volume as in most of the volumes of the series is on the factors of political and governmental administration more than on ethnic and national cultural factors.

88. KJELLÉN, RUDOLF, *Der Staat als Lebensform*, 4th ed., translated from the Swedish by J. Sandmeier (Berlin, 1924), Kurt Vowinkel.
Chapter III, pp. 87-135, deals with "Der Staat als Volk," the part of Kjellén's system which is known as *Ethnopolitik* or *Demopolitik*. The nation is described as an "ethnic individual" usually created by the forces of state and the relation of the political state to the nationality is dis-

cussed in this light. The author is the founder of the science of *Geopolitik*.

89. HAUSHOFER, KARL, *Geopolitik der Pan-Ideen* (Berlin, 1931), "Weltpolitische Bücherei," Vol. XXI, Zentral Verlag, 95 pp.
A geographical analysis of pan-movements in Asia, Africa, Australia, Europe and America.
Cf. No. 3.

90. LASKI, HAROLD JOSEPH, *A Grammar of Politics* (London, 1925), Allen and Unwin, 672 pp.
Chapter VI, pp. 218–40, deals with "Nationalism and Civilization." The conflict of nationalism with the modern world aspects of industrialism and its place in fostering war lead the author to a rejection of the concept of the nation state and to a pluralistic conception of loyalties.

91. LASKI, HAROLD JOSEPH, *Nationalism and the Future of Civilization* (London, 1932), Watts and Co., 64 pp.
A plea for international-mindedness as a check to national aggressive expansion.

92. REDSLOB, ROBERT, *Le Principe des nationalités. Les Origines, les fondements psychologiques, les forces adverses, les solutions possibles* (Paris, 1930), Recueil Sirey, 276 pp.
The body of the book is concerned with the juristic and administrative effects of nationalism and nationalist problems. The introductory section on the philosophy and psychology of nationalism is shallow and based wholly on other writers.

93. HEYKING, ALPHONS DE, *La Conception de l'état et l'idée de la cohésion ethnique. Le Point de vue du droit publique et des gens* (Paris, 1927), Rousseau, x, 155 pp.
This is chiefly a compilation of views of various other authors.

NATIONALISM AND ECONOMIC AFFAIRS

See also Nos. 3, 151, 199, 214, 215, 251, 293, 295, 296, 297, 303, 320a, 358, 359, 360, 377, 384, 393.

94. DELAISI, FRANCIS, *Political Myths and Economic Realities*, translated from the French (London, 1927), Noel Douglas, 409 pp.
This is brilliant critique of nationalism. The author pictures the conflict between the *homo economicus*, who acts internationally, and the *homo politicus*, who thinks nationally. Nationality, he holds, is an agrarian myth whereby concepts previously applied to the individual's land are now applied to the public domain.

95. SULZBACH, WALTER, *Nationales Gemeinschaftsgefühl und wirtschaftliches Interesse* (Leipzig, 1929), C. L. Hirschfeld, 152 pp.
An essay directed against the Marxist theory of economic causes of national imperialism.
Cf. Trotsky, Leon, "Nationalism and Economic Life," in *Foreign Affairs*, XII (1934), 395–402.

96. MISES, LUDWIG, *Nation, Staat und Wirtschaft. Beiträge zur Politik und Geschichte der Zeit* (Vienna, 1919), Manzsche Verlag, 182 pp.
This is a theoretical analysis of nationality in which the author bases nationality on language, even allowing for dual nationality for bilingualists. The author, a thoroughgoing and consistent economic and political liberal, analyzes economic nationalism, socialism and imperialism. He urges the extension of the principles of economic liberalism to political and international affairs.

97. MITSCHERLICH, WALDEMAR, *Nationalstaat und Nationalwirtschaft und ihre Zukunft*, 2d ed., (Leipzig, 1920), L. C. Hirschfeld, 51 pp.
A discussion of the conflict between nationalism and economic "universalism."

98. HOBSON, JOHN A., *Imperialism a Study*, 2d ed., (London, 1905), Constable, 408 pp.
The classic critique of imperialist economics and politics.

99. SCHNEE, HEINRICH, *Nationalismus und Imperialismus* (Berlin, 1928), Reimar Hobbing, xvi, 375 pp.
The development and relations of nationalism and imperialism in the British Empire, the United States of America, Japan, Russia, France and Italy. The author is concerned chiefly with the practical question of nationalism as a source of conflict.

100. FURNISS. EDGAR S., *The Position of the Laborer in a System of Nationalism* (Boston, 1920), Houghton Mifflin Co., 260 pp.
This Hart, Schaffner and Marx Prize Essay is a study of the labor theories of the later English mercantilists from 1660 to 1775. This period, the author holds, is similar to the period of revival of nationalism after the World War. He deals with the reaction of nationalism upon the life of labor and his conclusion is that "mercantilism teaches us that in working out a system of public policy based upon nationalistic purposes, the dominant class will attempt to bind the burden upon the shoulders of those groups whose political power is too slight to defend them from exploitation and will find justification for its policies in the plea of national necessity."

101. PAGE, KIRBY, *Dollars and World Peace* (New York, 1927), George H. Doran, vi, 214 pp.
Chapter I, pp. 9–43, gives an exposition of the thesis that war is caused by the exploitation of the concepts of national interest, national sovereignty, national honor and national patriotism.

102. GILL, CONRAD, *National Power and Prosperity, a Study of the Economic Causes of Modern Warfare* (London, 1927), T. Fisher Unwin, xxvii, 181 pp.
First published in 1916, this work reflects the war spirit in identifying Germany with all the evils of nationalism. It does, however, contain some general illuminating ideas by an economic liberal on the dangers of neo-mercantilism and economic nationalism and the concept of "national interests."

103. CULBERTSON, WILLIAM S., "Raw Materials and Foodstuffs in the Commercial Policies of Nations," in American Academy of Political and Social Science, *Annals*, CXII (1924), 1–145.
A discussion of national economic rivalry and economic imperialism, and a plea for national safety through international organization.

104. DELLE-DONNE, O., *European Tariff Policies since the War* (New York, 1928), Adelphi Company, xiv, 298 pp.
The author shows the influence of the postwar wave of nationalism in the policy of protective tariffs and the development of a new economic nationalism.

NATIONALISM, SOCIALISM AND COMMUNISM

See also Nos. 50, 95, 96, 130, 244, 245, 246, 252, 399, 405, 406, 418, 422, 430.

105. RENNER, KARL, *Das Selbstbestimmungsrecht der Nationen in besonderer Anwendung auf Österreich* (Vienna, 1918), Vol. I, *Nation und Staat*, Franz Deuticke, 294 pp.
This is the second revised edition of *Der Kampf der oesterreichischen Nationen um den Staat*, published under the pseudonym of Rudolf Springer in 1902. It is the fundamental theoretical exposition of the doctrine of national autonomy by a leading Austro-Marxist, with a profound philosophical analysis of the concepts of nationality and national state, together with a detailed program for administrative reform of the state to allow for national autonomy.
Cf. also No. 49.

106. BAUER, OTTO, *Die Nationalitätenfrage und die Sozialdemokratie*, 2d ed., (Vienna, 1924), Wiener Volksbuchhandlung, xxx, 576 pp. "Marx Studien," Vol. II.
This is the most thoroughgoing Socialist analysis of the problem of nationality. The author, the leading theoretician of the Austro-Marxists, takes a stand against the Socialists who fight nationalism by denying its existence. He defines a nation as a *Charaktergemeinschaft* grown out of a *Schicksalgemeinschaft*, and national character as an outcome of a historical process of the past, subject to change through the succeeding historical process. He thus traces the development of nationalism to economic transformations and changes in social structure. During the feudal and early capitalist epochs, only the ruling classes could be constituted as a *Kulturgemeinschaft*. Only the full development of capitalism brought the great masses into this process. The section of the book on the practical political problems concerning nationalities in Austria-Hungary (the book was first published in 1907) is now in most respects out of date, but it has historical significance in the influence it exerted on the development of the principle of cultural autonomy.
Cf. also Nos. 10, 49, 107.

107. KAUTSKY, KARL, "Nationalität und Internationalität" (Stuttgart, 1908), Ergänzungsheft No. 1 of *Neue Zeit*.
This work is directed against the stand of Otto Bauer (see No. 106). Nationality is conceived as a *Sprachgemeinschaft* and the author denies any such thing as national character. He advocates an antinational attitude for workers and holds that class interests are a greater bond than national interests.

108. CUNOW, HEINRICH, *Die Marxsche Geschichts-Gesellschafts und Staatstheorie*, 2 vols. (Berlin, 1920–21), Buchhandlung Vorwärts, Vol. II, Ch. I, pp. 9–50.
This is an exposition, by a right-wing Social-Democrat of the views of Marx and Engels on nationality. He argues that both Marx and Engels had a positive attitude toward nationality, although they did not believe in national self-determination. Their support of oppressed nationalities was dictated by general political conditions. The author's polemics are directed chiefly against Kautsky, (see No. 107).
See also PRIBRAM, K., "Deutscher Nationalismus und deutscher Sozialismus," in *Archiv für Sozialwissenschaft und Sozialpolitik*, XLIX (1932), 298–376.

109. HELLER, HERMANN, *Sozialismus und Nation*, 2d ed. (Berlin, 1931), Rowohlt Verlag, 107 pp.
This is a brilliant social interpretation of the development of German national feeling. It is an analysis of nationalism as a *Kulturgemeinschaft* and an attempt to harmonize this with socialist theory and practice.

110. LENIN, N., *Über die nationale Frage*, 2 vols. (Berlin, 1930–31), Verlag der Jugendinternationale, 116 pp. and 92 pp.; "Quellenbücher des Leninismus," Vols. IV–V.
Extracts from various speeches, articles and pamphlets by Lenin on the subject of nationalism, with a reprint of Joseph Stalin's "Der Leninismus und die nationale Frage" in place of an introduction.
Cf. also No. 244.

110a. STALIN, JOSEPH, *Leninism*, translated by Eden and Cedar Paul, 2d ed., 2 vols. (London, 1932–33), Allen and Unwin, 472 pp. and 468 pp.
The materials contained in these volumes may more properly be classed as "source materials of nationalism" and statements of public policy. In view, however, of the scarcity of objective scholarly material on the relations between Communism and nationalism, and also in view of the position of the author, these volumes are included here. The sections on "The National Question," Vol. I, pp. 135–44, "The Nationalist Question in Yugoslavia," Vol. I, pp. 259–64, "Political Tasks of the University of the Peoples of the East," Vol. I, pp. 267–82, "The Nationalist Question Once More," Vol. I, pp. 285–92, deal more immediately with the problem of nationalism and its relation to Communism and the policy of the Soviet Union.
Cf. also Nos. 110, 244.

NATIONALISM, EDUCATION AND PROPAGANDA

See also Nos. 58, 208, 274, 276, 277, 311, 312, 342, 344, 351, 373, 374, 375, 390, 398.

111. REISNER, EDWARD HARTMANN, *Nationalism in Education since 1789* (New York, 1922), Macmillan, xii, 575 pp.
This is a survey of the influence of nationalism on the educational systems of France, Prussia and the German Empire, England, and the United States, since the French Revolution. Written by an educator, the emphasis is mainly on institutional aspects. There are good accounts of all the important educational legislative acts.

112. KANDEL, I. L., editor, *Educational Yearbook of the International Institute of Teachers College, Columbia University, 1929* (New York, 1930), Teachers College, Columbia University, xiv, 559 pp.
Contributions on the philosophy underlying the national systems of education: on England, by Michael Sadler and Fred Clarke; on France, by Félix Pécaut; on Germany, by Aloys Fischer; on Italy, by E. Codignola; on Japan, by Kumaji Yoshida; and on the United States, by I. L. Kandel.

113. SCOTT, JONATHAN FRENCH, *The Menace of Nationalism in Education* (London, 1926), Allen and Unwin, 223 pp.
A study of nationalist indoctrination through school textbooks in England, France and Germany.

114. SCOTT, JONATHAN FRENCH, *Patriots in the Making. What America Can Learn from France and Germany* (New York, 1916), D. Appleton and Co., xv, 263 pp.

Although a preparedness-propaganda war book, it contains some valuable material on nationalist influence in education in Germany and France.

115. SALMON, LUCY MAYNARD, *The Newspaper and Authority* (New York, 1923), Oxford University Press, xxix, 505 pp.
Chapters XI–XIV contain good material on the use of the press as a means of propagating nationalism.

NATIONAL MINORITIES AND NATIONAL AUTONOMY

See also Nos. 2, 3, 7, 50, 52, 56, 221, 223, 244, 245, 411, 413.

116. AMMENDE, EWALD, editor, *Die Nationalitäten in den Staaten Europas* (Vienna, 1931), Wilhelm Braumüller, xxiv, 568 pp.
This is a very useful handbook concerning the various national minority groups in each of the European states, with full information on administrative, political, economic, educational and cultural aspects of the problems. It was published under the auspices of the Congress of European Nationalities.

117. WINKLER, WILHELM, *Statistisches Handbuch der europäischen Nationalitäten* (Vienna, 1931), Wilhelm Braumüller, vii, 248 pp.
This work contains comprehensive population statistics of the nationalities in Europe, arranged according to political states.

117a. MACARTNEY, C. A., *National States and National Minorities* (London, 1934), Oxford University Press, ix, 553 pp.
This is a most exhaustive study of the entire problem of national minorities, both in its historical aspects and in the various attempts at solution within the framework of the League of Nations, within the theoretically unnational state of the Soviet Union, and within the British Empire. It also includes a long introductory section on the historical origins of modern nationalism.

118. JUNGHANN, OTTO, *National Minorities in Europe* (New York, 1932), Covici Friede, 121 pp.
A competent introduction to the question of national minorities.

119. WOLZENDORFF, KURT, *Grundgedanken des Rechts der nationalen Minderheiten*, edited by Johannes Tiedje (Berlin, 1921), H. R. Engelmann, 46 pp.
This is one of the best philosophical analyses of the problem of national minorities and its relation to democracy, international law and social conditions.

120. ERLER, GEORG H. J., *Das Recht der nationalen Minderheiten* (Munich, 1931), Aschendorff, xvii, 530 pp. "Deutschtum und Ausland," Heft XXXVII–XXXIX.
This is one of the best general surveys of the minorities problem. Part I is a sociological survey of the nation and state problem; Part II, a historical and political survey from the Thirty Years' War to the World War, tracing the changes from religious to national minorities; Part III deals with the juristic elements. The author applies the subjective criteria of nationality also to minorities.

121. MAIR, ERICH, *Die Psychologie der nationalen Minderheit* (Münster, 1933), Aschendorff, 86 pp. "Deutschtum und Ausland," Heft LI.
This is an attempt at a social psychological study of the structure and reactions of a minority, particularly to the state, to its own national group, to other minorities, to the church, and to the League of Nations.

122. TRAMPLER, KURT, *Staaten und nationale Gemeinschaften. Eine Lösung des europäischen Minderheiten-Problems* (Munich, 1929), R. Oldenbourg, xii, 141 pp.
    The first part is a historical survey of the origins of the modern nationality problem, and the author finds the basic source in the state omnipotence since the French Revolution. The second part concerns the international guarantee of minority rights, and the author criticizes the treaties for being concerned only with individuals and not with groups. The third part contains a program for the solution of the national question, based on the full recognition of national groups.

123. TRAMPLER, KURT, *Die Krise des Nationalstaats. Das Nationalitätenproblem im neuen Europa* (Munich, 1932), Knorr und Hirth, 163 pp.
    An attack on the disposition of the nationality problem by the Versailles treaty. He shows the futility of boundary revisions as a solution, and the inadequacy of the idea of a national state. His proposals are the same as those of the congress of nationalities. The book also contains a section on the status of each of the important national minorities in Europe.

HISTORICAL AND REGIONAL STUDIES

NATIONALISM IN THE ANCIENT AND MEDIEVAL WORLD

See also Nos. 133, 143.

124. MÜHL, MAX, *Die antike Menschheitsidee in ihrer geschichtlichen Entwicklung* (Leipzig, 1928), Dieterichsche Verlagsbuchhandlung, 144 pp. "Das Erbe der Alten," Second Series, Vol. XIV.
    This is the best study of international and universal ideals in the ancient world.
    Cf. also Harris, Hugh, "Greek Origins of the Idea of Cosmopolitanism," in *International Journal of Ethics*, XXXVIII (1927–28), 1–10.

125. JÜTHNER, JULIUS, *Hellenen und Barbaren. Aus der Geschichte des Nationalbewusstseins* (Leipzig, 1923), Dieterichsche Verlagsbuchhandlung, 165 pp. "Das Erbe der Alten," Second Series, Vol. VIII.
    A discussion of the consciousness of nationality in the ancient world, as revealed in the distinction between the concepts of Hellenes and Barbarians. Plato, Aristotle, Macedonian imperialism, Isocrates, the Roman world, early Christianity and the Byzantine world are considered in this connection.

126. HETTICK, ERNEST L., *A Study in Ancient Nationalism. The Testimony of Euripides* (Williamsport, 1933), The Bayard Press, 72 pp.
    An illuminating approach to the problem of nationalism in antiquity through the works of Euripides.
    Cf. also Walek-Czernecki, T., "Le rôle de la nationalité dans l'histoire de l'antiquité," in International Committee of Historical Sciences, *Bulletin*, II (1929–30), 303–20.

127. HEISSENBÜTTEL, KURT H. T., *Die Bedeutung der Bezeichnungen für "Volk" und "Nation" bei den Geschichtsschreibern des 10. bis 13. Jahrhunderts* (Göttingen, 1920), Vandenhoeck und Ruprecht, 128 pp.
    A study of nationalist terminology in medieval historical writing.

128. WALLACH, RICHARD, *Das abendländische Gemeinschaftsbewusstsein im Mittelalter* (Leipzig, 1928), B. G. Teubner, 58 pp. "Beitrage zur Kulturgeschichte des Mittelalters und der Renaissance," Vol. XXXIV.
    The feeling of kinship of Western peoples as opposed to the Orient is

treated as well as the beginnings of national differentiation in Europe during the Middle Ages.

Cf. also Handelsmann, Marcel, "Le Rôle de la nationalité dans l'histoire du moyen age," in International Committee of Historical Sciences, *Bulletin*, II (1929), 235–47; and above all, Hugelmann, Karl Gottfried, "Mittelalterliches und modernes Nationalitätenproblem," in *Zeitschrift für Politik*, XIX (1930), 734–42, in which the author attacks the thesis that the nationality problem is only a modern phenomenon.

129. POWERS, GEORGE CORNELIUS, *Nationalism at the Council of Constance, 1414–1418* (Washington, 1927), Catholic University of America, xv, 208 pp.
The author traces the influence of the new nationalistic spirit in the organization of the Council of Constance, especially as regards the adoption of the new method of voting according to nations, and the factional strife. The study lacks integrated treatment.

MODERN NATIONALISM IN THE WEST

GENERAL HISTORICAL SURVEYS

See also Nos. 5, 7, 8, 49, 55, 117a, 122.

130. HAYES, CARLTON JOSEPH HUNTLEY, *The Historical Evolution of Modern Nationalism* (New York, 1931), Richard R. Smith, viii, 327 pp.
Emphasizing the fact that nationalism is plural rather than singular, the author considers the doctrines and political philosophies of five different types of nationalism which have developed in Europe since the eighteenth century. He takes up humanitarian nationalism as represented by Bolingbroke in England, Herder in Germany and Rousseau in France; Jacobin nationalism as found in the French Revolution; the traditional nationalism of Burke in England, Bonald in France and Friedrich Schlegel in Germany; liberal nationalism exemplified by Bentham in England, Guizot in France, Welcker in Germany and Mazzini in Italy; integral nationalism developed in France by Comte, Taine, Barrès and Maurras, and by Fascist theorists in Italy. Economic factors in nationalism are considered, in which the attitude of Socialists to nationalism is discussed as are the nationalistic economic doctrines of Fichte, Friedrich List, Rodbertus and the Historical School in Germany.
A good summary of the author's views is found in the *Encyclopaedia of the Social Sciences*, XI (1933), 240–48.

131. GOOCH, GEORGE PEABODY, *Nationalism* (London, 1920), The Swarthmore Press, 127 pp.
A brief survey of national movements since the French Revolution, treating nationalism as the aspiration toward political emancipation and independence of a distinct cultural group. This work is colored very much by the postwar slogan of self-determination of peoples.

132. ROSE, J. HOLLAND, *Nationality in Modern History* (New York, 1916), Macmillan, xi, 202 pp.
This is superseded by later works. The author has a somewhat confused idea of nationalism and the work is marred also by the influence of the World War.
Cf. also Stephens, Henry Morse, "Nationality and History," in *American Historical Review*, XXI (1916), 225–36.

133. GIBBONS, HERBERT ADAMS, *Nationalism and Internationalism* (New York, 1930), F. A. Stokes, xi, 273 pp.
This is a very popular series of lectures on nationalist movements from earliest times to the present, by a strong American nationalist. He is decidedly opposed to the thesis that nationalism is an exclusively modern manifestation.

134. POLLARD, A. F., *Factors in Modern History* (London, 1926), T. and A. Constable, xi, 287 pp.
Chapter I, pp. 1–25, on "Nationality," brings out very clearly the modern character of nationalism.

135. DUNNING, WILLIAM ARCHIBALD, *A History of Political Theories from Rousseau to Spencer* (New York, 1920), Macmillan, ix, 446 pp.
Chapter VIII deals with the place of the idea of nationality in nineteenth century political theory.

136. HAUSER, HENRI, *Le Principe des nationalités, ses origines historiques* (Paris, 1916), Félix Alcan, 30 pp.
A very cursory survey of the concept of nationalism and its modern development. The author bases his view of nationality on the principle of collective will as developed also by Boutroux and Renan.

137. BOEHM, MAX HILDEBERT, *Europa irredenta. Eine Einführung in das Nationalitätenproblem der Gegenwart* (Berlin, 1923), Reimar Hobbing, 336 pp.
This is the work of a "young conservative" of the Ring group of Moeller van den Bruck. It is a brilliant history of modern nationalist movements revealing particularly a very intimate knowledge of Slavic and Central Europe. The author draws a distinction between German nationalism with its emphasis on culture and Western nationalism which, fused with the democratic principle, is essentially political and stems from the French revolution. The author is anti-French and filled with a strong passion against the Versailles treaty and the League of Nations and their treatment of the nationality problem.
Cf. also Koht, Haldvan, "L'Ésprit national et l'ideé de la souveraineté du peuple," in International Committee of Historical Sciences. *Bulletin*, II (1929–30), 217–24.

138. FOURNOL, ÉTIENNE, *Les Nations romantiques* (Paris, 1931), Éditions des Portiques, 253 pp.
The author distinguishes between romantic nationalism where the movement came out of romanticism, and the nationalism of the classic nations where nationalism was developed during the age of absolutism. The new nationalism is marked by democracy and traditionalism, and Germany, Italy and the Slavic nationalities are examples of this type. There are good characterizations of the nationalism of Herder, Fichte, and the Italian nationalism of Dante, Machiavelli, Mazzini, and Gioberti.

139. HELLER, HERMAN, *Politische Ideenkreise der Gegenwart* (Breslau, 1926), Ferdinand Hirt, 156 pp.
The author treats the growth and development of the national idea in its relation to liberalism and democracy. He traces the cultural nationalism of the eighteenth century, the national ideas of Fichte, Hegel, and the men of 1848, the work of Bismarck, and finally the racial and Teutonic nationalism of more recent times. His conclusion is that nationalism in Europe must receive some sort of counterpoise in the form of a European ideal.

140. WECHSSLER, EDUARD, *Ésprit und Geist* (Leipzig, 1927), Velhagen und Klasing, 604 pp.

This is a serious attempt at a comparison of French and German national cultures and intellectual reactions.

141. BRYCE, VISCOUNT, "The Principle of Nationality and Its Applications," in *Essays and Addresses in War Time* (New York, 1918), Macmillan, pp. 140–75.
A war-time essay on the principle of nationality and the nationality problems presented to the Peace Conference in all parts of the world.

NATIONALISM IN GERMANY AND AUSTRIA

See also Nos. 4, 7, 9, 18, 24, 46, 48, 81, 109, 111, 112, 113, 114, 140.

For the historical development of German nationalism, the writings of the following are important: the philologists, Jakob and Wilhelm Grimm; the litterateurs, Ernst Moritz Arndt, Novalis, Friedrich and August Wilhelm Schlegel, Joseph Görres, Paul Lagarde and Richard Wagner; the political philosophers, Johann Kaspar Bluntschli, Houston Stewart Chamberlain, Johann Gottlieb Fichte, Heinrich Rudolph Gneist, Ludwig Gumplowicz, Georg Wilhelm Hegel, Johann Gottfried Herder, Wilhelm von Humboldt, Friedrich Karl von Moser, Adam Müller, Friedrich Karl Savigny, Friedrich Schleiermacher and Rudolf Steiner; the historians, Johann Gustav Droysen, Max Duncker, Friedrich Giesebrecht, Heinrich Luden, Theodor Mommsen, Barthold Niebuhr, Georg Heinrich Pertz, August Ludwig Schlözer, Heinrich von Sybel, Heinrich von Treitschke and Georg Waitz; and the economist, Friedrich List.

142. JASTROW, I., *Geschichte des deutschen Einheitstraumes und seiner Erfüllung*, 4th ed. (Berlin, 1891), Allgemeiner Verein für Deutsche Literatur, viii, 400 pp.
One of the best of the older works, dealing with the growth of the idea of a unified national German state and concerned exclusively with political nationalism.

143. JOACHIMSEN, PAUL, *Vom deutschen Volk zum deutschen Staat. Eine Geschichte des deutschen Nationalbewusstseins* (Leipzig, 1916), B. G. Teubner, 130 pp.
Although inspired by patriotic motives during the World War, this book gives a good popular survey of the growth of German national feeling from earliest times to the present. It is marked by a strong Protestant feeling.
See also Joachimsen, Paul, "Zur historischen Psychologie des deutschen Staatsgedankens," in *Die Dioskuren*, I (1922), 160–77, and Hugelmann, K. G., "Die deutsche Nation und der deutsche Nationalstaat im Mittelalter," in *Historisches Jahrbuch*, LI (1931), 1–29, 445–84.

144. PINSON, KOPPEL S., *Pietism as a Factor in the Rise of German Nationalism* (New York, 1934), Columbia University Press, 227 pp. "Studies in Economics, History and Public Law," No. 398.
The author aims to show that the religious emotions, psychological reactions and intellectual ideas engendered in the Pietist movement came, in the process of secularization, to be transferred to the nationality. He traces this process from the times of Spener and Francke, through the Moravian Brethren and Zinzendorf, to the "enlightened Pietism" of Hamann, Lavater, Schleiermacher and Novalis.

145. MEINECKE, FRIEDRICH, *Weltbürgertum und Nationalstaat. Studien zur Genesis des deutschen Nationalstaates*, 7th ed. (Munich, 1928), R. Oldenbourg Verlag, x, 558 pp.
This is the classic work on the history of German nationalism. The first

part is concerned with the problem of the struggle between the universal aspects of cultural nationalism and cosmopolitanism and the national political idea, and how the latter triumphed. This is illustrated by monographic expositions of the national ideas of representative figures such as Wilhelm von Humboldt, Novalis, Friedrich Schlegel, Fichte, Adam Müller, Stein, Gneisenau, Hardenberg, Haller, Hegel, Ranke and Bismarck. The second part of the book deals with the Prussian–German question and the triumph of the Prussian idea. It centers chiefly around the figures of 1848, but carries the discussion down to Bismarck and, in the seventh edition, includes an essay on the same problem in the establishment of the Weimar Republic. Cf. No. 10.

146. Schnabel, Franz, *Deutsche Geschichte im neunzehnten Jahrhundert*, Vols. I–II (Freiburg, 1929–33), Herder.
A discussion of the transition from cosmopolitanism to nationalism, with special attention tó the Romanticists, is found in I, 283–315.

147. Natorp, Paul G., *Der Deutsche und sein Staat* (Erlangen, 1924), Verlag der Philosophischen Akademie, 120 pp.
'This contains an address, "Volk und Menschheit," and an essay "Vom Staat," in which the author takes up the relations between individual, nationality and humanity.

148. Molisch, Paul, *Geschichte der deutsch-nationalen Bewegung in Österreich von ihren Anfängen bis zum Zerfall der Monarchie* (Jena, 1926), G. Fischer, x, 277 pp.
The author traces the development of a national consciousness among the Germans in Austria-Hungary to the time of the World War. It is written from a nationalist conservative viewpoint.

149. Rapp, Adolph, *Der deutsche Gedanke, seine Entwicklung im politischen und geistigen Leben seit dem 18. Jahrhundert* (Bonn, 1920), Kurt Schroeder, 373 pp. "Bücherei der Kultur und Geschichte," Vol. VIII.
The German idea is identified with the strong political *Machtstaat*. This book is a strongly nationalistic account of the evolution of the idea, is strongly prejudiced, and is for the most part unreliable.

150. Schmahl, Eugen, *Der Aufstieg der nationalen Idee* (Stuttgart, 1933), Union deutsche Verlagsgesellschaft, 222 pp.
A review of German nationalism as a background for the advent of National Socialism.

151. Andler, Charles, editor, *Collection de documents sur le pangermanisme*, 4 vols. (Paris, 1915–17), Louis Conrad.
These volumes are mainly extracts from German writers, given in French translation, with long introductions to each volume by the editor. Their general thesis is that Germany assumed the mission of organizing the world into an integrated humanity, and the materials in illustration of this are drawn from the works of German philosophers, poets and scholars since the time of Fichte. The work is to be used with great caution, as it was obviously inspired by World War conditions. Vol. I, *Les Origines du pangermanisme (1800 à 1888)*, lviii, 335 pp., contains extracts from Dietrich von Bülow, Ernst Moritz Arndt, Friedrich Ludwig Jahn, Friedrich List, Helmuth von Moltke, Bismarck, Treitschke, Paul de Lagarde and Constantin Frantz. Vol. II, *Le Pangermanisme continental sous Guillaume II (de 1888 à 1914)* xxxiii, 480 pp., contains texts on ecomonic nationalism from Julius von Eckardt, William II, Prince von Bülow, Paul Dehn, Friedrich Lange, Fritz Bley, Ernst Hasse, Count zu Reventlow, Albrecht Wirth, Paul Rohrbach and Maxmilian Harden. Vol. III, *Le Pangermanisme colonial sous Guillaume II (de 1888 à 1914)* c, 335 pp.,

contains extracts from Alfred Zimmerman, Karl von Stengel, Ferdinand Wohltmann, Bartholomäus von Werner, Bernhard Dernburg, Richard Kranel, Albert Schaeffle, Max Vosberg-Rekow, Friedrich Lange, Johannes Unold, Heinrich Class, Joachim von Bülow, Theodore Schiemann, Friedrich Naumann, Gerhard Hildebrand, Paul Rohrbach and Maximilian Harden. Vol. IV, *Le Pangermanisme philosophique (1800 à 1914)* clii, 398 pp., contains texts from Fichte, Hegel, Goerres, F. Schlegel, Friedrich Ratzel, Arthur Dix, Karl Lamprecht, Albrecht Wirth, Julius Langbehn, Friedrich Lange, Ludwig Woltmann, Heinrich Driesmans, H. S. Chamberlain, Joseph Ludwig Reimer, Klaus Wagner and Friedrich von Bernhardi.

152. CAPPIS, OSCAR BERNHARD, *Die Idee des Kleinstaates im Deutschland des 19. Jahrhunderts* (Basel, 1923), Franz Mehr, 203 pp.
A series of monographic studies on K. L. von Haller, Adam Müller, Friedrich Schlegel, Niebuhr, Rotteck, Carl Theodor Welcker, Gervinus, Constantin Frantz, Jakob Burckhardt, J. G. Droysen, Mommsen, R. von Mohl, J. K. Bluntschli and Treitschke, showing their views on the problem of local state versus unified German state, and federalism as an intermediate state.

153. ZEYDEL, E. H., *The Holy Roman Empire in German Literature* (New York, 1918), Columbia University Press, ix, 144 pp.
The Holy Roman Empire presented one of the major problems in the development of a German nationalism. This book deals with the attitude toward the Empire as expressed in German literature from earliest times to the age of Goethe and Fichte.
See also Berney, Arnold, "Reichstradition und Nationalstaatsgedanke (1789–1815)," in *Historische Zeitschrift.* CXL (1929), 57–86; and No. 155.

154. FRANCKE, KUNO, *Weltbürgertum in der deutschen Literatur von Herder bis Nietzsche* (Berlin, 1928), Weidmannsche Buchhandlung, 140 pp.
Volume III of his *Kulturwerte der deutschen Literatur.* This is a beautiful essay on the cosmopolitan strain in German literature of the nineteenth century, which, however, proved to be a very weak counterpoise to the stronger nationalist strain.
Cf. Lenz, Max, "Deutsche Nationalempfinden im Zeitalter unserer Klassiker," in *Jahrbuch der Goethe Gesellschaft*, II (1915), 265–300.

155. RENNER, BRUNO, *Die nationalen Einigungsbestrebungen Friedrich Karl von Mosers, 1765–1767* (Königsberg, 1919), H. Schwarz, 103 pp.
Chiefly an analysis of Moser's *Von dem deutschen Nationalgeist, Reliquien*, and his *Patriotische Briefe.*

156. GERLACH, OTTO, *Die Idee der Nationalerziehung in der Geschichte der preussischen Volksschule.* Vol. I, *Die Nationalerziehung im 18. Jahrhundert, dargestellt an ihrem Hauptvertretter Rochow*, (Langensalza, 1932), J. Beltz, vii, 158 pp.
A study of the most important pioneer of public-school and national education in Germany.

157. HAY, JOSEPH, *Staat, Volk und Weltbürgerthum in den Berlinischen Monatschrift von Friedrich Gedicke und Johann Erich Biester (1783–96)* (Berlin, 1913), Haude und Spener, vi, 83 pp.
A doctoral dissertation dealing with a leading journal of the Berlin *Aufklärer* and the nationalist and cosmopolitan strains contained therein.

158. ERGANG, ROBERT R., *Herder and the Foundations of German Nationalism* (New York, 1931), Columbia University Press, 288 pp. "Studies in History, Economics and Public Law," No. 341.
An exhaustive study of the first modern theorist of nationalism. Herder's

nationalism is shown to be cultural and humanitarian, rather than political. The author has reconstructed from Herder's scattered writings Herder's conception of what constitutes a nationality, and he shows how Herder applied his doctrines more specifically to the general questions of language, literature and historical tradition, and their relations to German nationality. A useful general survey of German national feeling in the eighteenth century opens the volume, and a chapter on the subsequent influence of Herder's doctrines of nationalism, particularly among the Slavs, Hungarians, and on Mazzini, brings the work to a close. The lengthy quotations from Herder are particularly valuable to the English reader since very little of Herder's writings has been translated into English. See also Hayes, Carlton J. H., "Contributions of Herder to the Doctrine of Nationalism," in *American Historical Review*, XXXII (1927), 719–36.

159. GOEKEN, WALTHER, *Herder als Deutscher: ein literaturhistorischer Beitrag zur Entwicklung der deutschen Nationalidee* (Tübingen, 1926), Kohlhammer, 131 pp. "Tübingen Germanistische Arbeiten," Vol. I.
A poor attempt at an evaluation of the political and nationalistic elements in Herder, consisting mainly of quotations.

160. BASCH, VICTOR, *Les Doctrines politiques des philosophes classiques de l'Allemagne: Leibnitz, Kant, Fichte, Hegel* (Paris, 1927), Alcan, x, 336 pp.
The author refutes the contention of Boutroux and others that extreme German nationalism, as developed during and after the war, stems from the great idealist philosophers. He compares German idealism to French Jacobinism and emphasizes its humanitarian character.

161. BORRIES, KURT, *Kant als Politiker. Zur Staats– und Gesellschaftslehre des Kritizismus* (Leipzig, 1928), Felix Meiner, vii, 248 pp.
Kant's views on nation and national feeling are discussed in Ch. III, Part IV, pp. 200–34.
Cf. Meyer, Friedrich, "Über Kants Stellung zu Nation und Staat," in *Historische Zeitschrift*, CXXXIII (1926), 197–219.

162. HELLER, HERMANN, *Hegel und der nationale Machtstaatsgedanke in Deutschland* (Leipzig, 1921), Teubner, vi, 210 pp.
This is one of the most important studies of Hegel. The author traces the transition from the ideal of *Kulturstaat* to that of *Machtstaat* in Germany, and attributes it chiefly to the influence of Hegel. He presents a brilliant analysis of Hegel's political and national ideas and his influence on subsequent political thinkers.

163. DITTMANN, FRIEDRICH, *Der Begriff des Volksgeistes bei Hegel* (Leipzig, 1909), R. Voigtländer Verlag, vi, 108 pp. "Beiträge zur Kultur und Universal Geschichte," Heft X.
An able analysis of Hegel's concept of *Volksgeist*, or "spirit of a people," of how he applied it in historical practice, and a comparison with the views of Kant and Herder.

164. ENGELBRECHT, H. C., *Johann Gottlieb Fichte. A Study of his Writings with Special Reference to his Nationalism* (New York, 1933), Columbia University Press, 221 pp. "Studies in History Economics and Public Law," No. 383.
A fine presentation of Fichte's ideas of nationalism against the background of his general political, economic and social views. It is particularly valuable for its analysis of the nationalist contents of Fichte's individual works, and for the chapter on Fichte's influence in the nineteenth and twentieth centuries. It is weaker in relating Fichte to the general intellectual currents of his time.
See also No. 264; and Binder, Julius, "Fichte und die Nation," in *Logos*, X (1922), 275–315.

165. WALLNER, NICO, *Fichte als politischer Denker. Werden und Wesen seiner Gedanken über den Staat.* (Halle, 1926), M. Niemeyer, 280 pp.
The author wishes to show that Fichte cannot be claimed by Liberals, Social Democrats, Conservatives or Democrats, but that his political views can be understood only as part of his general religious, philosophical view. This religious, philosophical character he also finds in Fichte's nationalism. He substantiates Meinecke's thesis, however, that the national state which Fichte talks about in his *Reden* is not a practical political construct, but rather the dictate of a universally oriented humanitarian philosophy. Ch. V, pp. 189–220, is most important for the consideration of his nationalism.
Cf. No. 145.

166. LÉON, XAVIER, *Fichte et son temps,* 2 vols. in 3 (Paris, 1922–27), Armand Colin.
Vol. II, Part II, Chs. I–II, contains a detailed analysis of Fichte's *Patriotic Dialogues* and his *Addresses to the German Nation.*

167. REIDT, KONRAD, *Das Nationale und das Übernationale bei Fichte mit besonderer Berücksichtigung seiner Pädagogik* (Giessen, 1926), Privately printed, 87 pp.
Fichte's doctrines of nationalism are studied in relation to his general philosophic system. Fichte stands midway between the Enlightenment and Hegelianism. He recognizes the rights of individual personality, but claims that these rights can be attained only through community of national feeling. Special attention is devoted to his pedagogic views.

168. GOOCH, GEORGE PEABODY, *Germany and the French Revolution* (London, 1920), Longmans, Green and Co., vii, 543 pp.
This is a good work on the general influences of the French Revolution on German political and intellectual life. It is arranged in the form of monographic studies and is rather a collection of quotations than an integrated study. It does contain, however, a great deal of material on the effects of the Revolution in stimulating German and Prussian national consciousness.

169. STERN, ALFRED, *Der Einfluss der französischen Revolution auf das deutsche Geistesleben* (Stuttgart, 1928), J. G. Cotta, 248 pp.
The author's thesis is that the French Revolution was the primary cause in turning German intellectual life from cosmopolitanism to nationalism. This process is studied in the reactions of the leading poets, writers, philosophers and publicists of the period.

170. VERSCHOOR, A. D., *Die ältere deutsche Romantik und die Nationalidee* (Amsterdam, 1928), H. J. Paris, viii, 150 pp.
The influence of the early Romanticists, particularly the Schlegel brothers, on the turn from rationalist cosmopolitanism to German national patriotism.

171. KLUCKHOHN, PAUL, *Persönlichkeit und Gemeinschaft. Studien zur Staatsauffassung der deutschen Romantik.* (Halle, 1925), Max Niemeyer, 111 pp.
This work is chiefly concerned with the elements of nationalism and patriotism in German political philosophy of the eighteenth and early nineteenth centuries, contrasting the cosmopolitanism of the Enlightenment with the nationalism of the Romantic movements and its precursors. Most attention is paid to Novalis, Schleiermacher, Schelling, Friedrich Schlegel, Adam Müller and Heinrich von Kleist. The problem is discussed in relation to questions of the new historical sense, medievalism, etc.

172. BAXA, JAKOB, *Einführung in die romantische Staatswissenschaft,* 2d ed. (Jena, 1931), Gustav Fischer, xv, 295 pp. "Ergänzungsbände zur Sammlung Herdflamme," Vol. IV.

This book contains a discussion of the nationalist doctrines of the German Romanticists, particularly Fichte, Novalis, Friedrich Schlegel and Adam Müller, by an enthusiastic and uncritical Neo-Romanticist and disciple of Othmar Spann.

173. SCHMITT, CARL, *Politische Romantik*, 2d ed. (Munich, 1925), Duncker und Humblot, 123 pp.

A thoroughly realistic analysis of German Romantic political philosophy, concerned chiefly with Adam Müller, attempting to show the utter barrenness and lack of originality in Romantic political ideas and denying any contributions of Romanticism to national or historical feeling.

See the review of the first edition of this book by Friedrich Meinecke in *Historische Zeitschrift*, CXXI (1920), 292–96.

174. BORRIES, KURT, *Die Romantik und die Geschichte. Studien zur romantischen Lebensform* (Berlin, 1925), Deutsche Verlagsgesellschaft für Politik und Geschichte, 235 pp.

A balanced and moderate treatment of the Romantic philosophy of history and the concept of *Volksgeist*.

175. SALOMON, GOTTFRIED, *Das Mittelalter als Ideal in der Romantik* (Munich, 1922), Drei Masken Verlag, 127 pp.

A good discussion of medievalism as a factor in Romantic nationalism.

176. SAMUEL, RICHARD, *Die poetische Staats- und Geschichtsauffassung Friedrich von Hardenbergs* (Frankfurt, 1925), Diesterweg, 302 pp. "Deutsche Forschungen," Vol. XII.

This is the best study of the political doctrines of Novalis with considerable attention to the place of nationality and a very good discussion of the medievalism of Novalis.

177. BRANDT, OTTO, *A. W. Schlegel. Der Romantiker und die Politik* (Stuttgart, 1919), Deutsche Verlagsanstalt, viii, 258 pp.

An attempt to show how German national feeling overcame universalism. Schlegel is pictured as one of the first political Romanticists and the first to espouse the cause of the medieval feudal state. It is a good treatment of Schlegel in the setting of his times and makes use of much unpublished material.

178. VOLPERS, RICHARD, *Friedrich Schlegel als politischer Denker und deutscher Patriot* (Berlin, 1917), B. Behrs Verlag, x, 250 pp.

The author discusses Schlegel's attitude toward the state, people and nationality. He aims to show that Schlegel comprehended the idea of a national state more deeply than did Schleiermacher.

179. WIENEKE, ERNST, *Patriotismus und Religion in Friedrich Schlegels Gedichten* (Dresden, 1913), Albert Hille, 104 pp.

A brief discussion of Schlegel's political and national ideas and their expression in his poetic works.

180. MÜSEBECK, ERNST, *Schleiermacher in der Geschichte der Staatsidee und des Nationalbewusstseins* (Berlin, 1927), Reimar Hobbing, 150 pp.

A genetic study of Schleiermacher's political philosophy of nationalism and his patriotic activity, emphasizing particularly the Protestant character of his ideas.

See also Reuter, H., "Schleiermachers Stellung zur Idee der Nation und des nationalen Staates," in *Theologische Studien und Kritiken*, XXI (1918), 439–504; Reinhard, J., "Friedrich Schleiermacher als deutscher Patriot," in *Neue Jahrbücher für Pädagogik*, IV (1899), 345–60; Dilthey, W., "Schleiermachers politische Gesinnung und Wirksamkeit," in *Preussische Jahrbücher*, X (1862), 234–77; and No. 144.

181. BAUER, JOHANNES, *Schleiermacher als politischer Prediger. Ein Beitrag zur Geschichte der nationalen Erhebung vor hundert Jahren* (Giessen,

1908), Töpelmann, xii, 364 pp. "Studien zur Geschichte des neueren Protestantismus," Heft IV.
The best and most elaborate analysis of Schleiermacher's patriotic sermons.

182. UNGERN-STERNBERG, ARTHUR VON, *Schleiermachers völkische Botschaft. Aus der Zeit der deutschen Erneuerung* (Gotha, 1933), Leopold Klotz, 251 pp.
A theologically colored interpretation of Schleiermacher's nationalist doctrines as revealed in his political, pedagogic and religious writings.

183. UHLMANN, JOHANNES, *Joseph Görres und die deutsche Einheits- und Verfassungsfrage bis zum Jahre 1824* (Leipzig, 1912), Quelle und Meyer, x, 155 pp. "Leipziger Historische Abhandlungen," Heft XXXII.
On the background of his general political and philosophic ideas, the author traces Görres's theories and nationalist activities as publicist between 1814 and 1819.

184. RUTH, PAUL HERMANN, *Arndt und die Geschichte* (Munich, 1930), R. Oldenbourg, xxviii, 188 pp. *Historische Zeitschrift*, Beiheft XVIII.
The most complete analysis of Arndt's social, political and historical ideas, particularly illuminating in revealing the clash between cosmopolitanism and nationalism, individualism and social feeling, Swedish and German patriotism, and the final victory of German national feeling. It also includes a good account of Arndt's influence on nationalist historical writing.

185. RITTER, GERHARD, *Stein, eine politische Biographie.* Vol. I, *Der Reformer;* Vol. II, *Der Vorkämpfer nationaler Freiheit und Einheit,* (Stuttgart, 1931), Deutsche Verlagsanstallt, xi, 542 pp., and 408 pp.
Ritter takes issue with Meinecke's interpretation of Stein's nationalism. He denies any element of universal cosmopolitanism in Stein's ideas, which Meinecke attributes to eighteenth-century influence and which thus distinguishes him from the policy of the *Realpolitik* of Bismarck. Cf. the review by Otto Hintze in *Historische Zeitschrift*, CXLVI (1932), 354–55; and that by Hans Rothfels in the *Deutsche Literaturzeitung*, LIII (1932), 742–56.
See also Drüner, H., "Der nationale und der universale Gedanke bei dem Freiherrn vom Stein," in *Historische Vierteljahrschrift*, XXII (1924–25), 28–69.

186. ANTONOWYTSCH, MICHAEL, *Friedrich Ludwig Jahn. Ein Beitrag zur Geschichte der Anfange des deutschen Nationalismus* (Berlin, 1933), Emil Ebering, 82 pp. "Historische Studien," No. CCXXX.
An interpretation of Jahn as an opponent of liberalism, showing the influence of the French Revolution in his emphasis on *Volk*, and of the Romantic movement in his emotionalism. The author emphasizes Jahn's importance as the first great popularizer of nationalism among the masses.

187. PREUSS, GEORG FRIEDRICH, *Die Quellen des Nationalgeistes der Befreiungskriege* (Berlin, 1914), Ernst Siegfried Mittler, 74 pp.
The author shows the interaction of the spirit of Frederick the Great, the classic spirit of civic duty, Romanticism with its national emphasis, and the philosophy of Fichte, to produce the national spirit of 1813.

188. GROMMAIRE, G., *La Littérature patriotique en Allemagne, 1800–1815* (Paris, 1911), A. Colin, viii, 305 pp.
A very able study of patriotism in German literature up to 1815. It is concerned more with patriotism than with nationalism and also places more emphasis on the literary than on the general intellectual and philosophic currents. It is nevertheless the best book on the subject and is quite objective.

189. CHUQUET, ARTHUR, *Les Chants patriotiques de l'Allemagne, 1813–1918* (Paris, 1920), Ernest Leroux, 316 pp.
A patriotic Frenchman studies the propagation of German patriotism in the German poetry of the nineteenth century.

190. HAUPT, HERMANN and PAUL WENTZCKE, editors, *Quellen und Darstellungen zur Geschichte der Burschenschaft und der deutschen Einheitsbewegung*, Vols. I–XIII (Heidelberg, 1910–32), Carl Winters.
A collection of studies by various German scholars on the *Burschenschaft* movement. Of particular importance is the general history of the *Burschenschaft* by Paul Wentzcke and Georg Heer in Vols. VI, X and XI, and the study of the German national colors by Paul Wentzcke in Vol. IX.

191. LANGSAM, WALTER C., *The Napoleonic Wars and German Nationalism in Austria* (New York, 1930), Columbia University Press, vii, 243 pp. "Studies in History, Economics and Public Law," No. 324.
The author considers a phase of German nationalism which has received but scant treatment, most of the attention having been given to Prussia. The work makes abundant use of manuscript and archive material and is particularly valuable in showing the use of nationalist propaganda consciously set in motion by the government through the press, theater, and pamphlets. The spread of nationalism among the masses is shown in folk songs. The book closes with a good summary of the views of Metternich on nationalism, and the effects on the resulting settlement of the German situation. It is weak, however, in the treatment of the background and fails to take into account the work of Joseph II and the relations of Austro-German nationalism to the larger German question.

191a. ROBERT, ANDRÉ, *L'Idée nationale autrichienne et les guerres de Napoléon; l'apostolat du Baron de Hormayr et le salon de Caroline Pichler* (Paris, 1933), *Félix Alcan*, ix, 604 pp.
The author treats of the influence of the French Revolution in stimulating Austrian national consciousness in the period 1805-9, and of the chief inspirer of this movement, Baron Hormayr.

192. ULBRICHT, WALTHER, *Bunsen und die deutsche Einheitsbewegung* (Leipzig, 1910), Quelle und Meyer, xii, 146 pp. "Leipziger Historische Abhandlungen," Heft XX.
The views on German national unity of Christian Karl Josias von Bunsen, one of the important leaders of 1848.

193. DE JONGE, A. R., *Gottfried Kinkel as a Political and Social Thinker* (New York, 1926), Columbia University Press, xvi, 156 pp.
The political and nationalist theories of an 1848 Republican poet and patriot.

194. SCHROTH, HAUSGEORG, *Welt– und Staatsideen des deutschen Liberalismus in der Zeit der Einheits– und Freiheitskämpfe, 1859–1866. Ein Beitrag zur Soziologie des deutschen politischen Denkens.* (Berlin, 1931), Emil Ebering, 120 pp. "Historische Studien," No. CCI.
A poor attempt to analyze the political ideas of liberalism during the unification period and to show how little influence liberalism had.

195. FENSKE, WALTER, *J. G. Droysen und das deutsche Nationalstaats-problem. Ein Beitrag zur Geschichte der Frankfurter Nationalversammlung von 1848-49* (Erlangen, 1930), Palm und Enke, vii, 244 pp. "Erlanger Abhandlungen zur mittleren und neueren Geschichte," Vol. II.
This work is concerned mainly with Droysen's ideas and the rôle played by him during the period of the Frankfurt Assembly of 1848–49, the influence of Hegel, and the evolution of his "Prussian" views.

196. GILBERT, FELIX, *J. G. Droysen und die preussische-deutsche Problem* (Munich, 1931), R. Oldenbourg, iv, 148 pp. *Historische Zeitschrift,* Beiheft XX.
This study shows the transformation of Droysen from a federalist before 1848 to a most ardent advocate of Prussian hegemony.

197. GASPARIAN, ASCHOT, *Der Begriff der Nation in der deutschen Geschichtsschreibung des 19. Jahrhunderts* (Leipzig, 1916), R. Voigtländers Verlag, viii, 64 pp. "Beiträge zur Kultur und Universal Geschichte," Heft XXXVIII.
An analysis of the use of the concept of the nation in the historical writings of Ranke, Treitschke, Sybel, Droysen and Lamprecht.

197a. SCHMIDT, HERBERT, *Friedrich Julius Stahl und die deutsche Nationalstaatsidee* (Berlin, 1914), M. and H. Marcus, viii, 106 pp. "Historische Untersuchungen," Heft IV.
The views of the theoretical founder of Prussian conservatism on German political nationalism.

198. KATSCH, HILDEGARD, *Heinrich von Treitschke und die preussisch-deutsche Frage von 1860–1864* (Munich, 1919), R. Oldenbourg, 71 pp.
The author discusses Treitschke's nationalist views as revealed in his attitude toward domestic affairs in Prussia, 1860–63, his view of the rôle of Prussia in German unification and his position on the Schleswig-Holstein problem.

199. SOMMER, ARTUR, *Friedrich Lists System der politischen Ökonomie* (Jena, 1927), Gustav Fischer, xii, 242 pp. "List Studien," Heft I.
This is the best study of the economic and political doctrines of Friedrich List, and gives special attention to List's economic nationalism.
See also Baasch, Ernst, "Die deutschen wirtschaftlichen Einheitsbestrebungen die Hansestädte und Friedrich List bis zum Jahre 1821," in *Historische Zeitschrift,* CXXII (1920), 454–85; and Albrecht, Gerhard, "Die Ausgestaltung des Listschen Nationalitätsprinzips durch Eugen Dühring," in *Zeitschrift für die gesamte Staatswissenschaft,* LXXXIII (1927), 1–32.

200. FRANZ, GÜNTHER, *Bismarcks Nationalgefühl,* (Leipzig, 1926), B. G. Teubner, vi, 125 pp.
This is the best study of the national ideas of Bismarck, and reveals the great Prussian hero as lacking any deep feeling of German nationalism. What guided him chiefly was a strong feeling for the political state, which found concrete expression in his Prussianism. The author tends to exaggerate the growth of Bismarck's national feeling toward the end of his life. Cf. the review by H. Ritter von Srbik in *Historische Zeitschrift,* CXXXVII (1928), 327–32.
See also Rothfels, Hans, "Bismarck und die Nationalitätenfragen des Ostens," in *Historische Zeitschrift,* CXLVII (1933), 89–105.

201. GAZLEY, J. G., *American Opinion of German Unification, 1848–71* (New York, 1926), Columbia University Press, 586 pp. "Studies in History, Economics and Public Law," No. 267.
A discussion of the attitude of American public opinion, as reflected in newspapers, periodicals and books, of the nationalist movement in Germany; of the movement of 1848, of the Austro-Prussian War and of the Franco-Prussian War. There is also a section on Hungary and France.

202. BREITLING, RICHARD, *Paul de Lagarde und der grossdeutsche Gedanke* (Vienna, 1927), Wilhelm Braumüller, viii, 116 pp.
A very sympathetic treatment of the nationalist doctrines of one of the most influential nationalist theorists of the late nineteenth century. It excels in placing Lagarde in the general setting of his times.

203. KLAMROTH, KURT, *Staat und Nation bei Paul de Lagarde. Ein Beitrag zur Geschichte der politischen Ideenlehre im 19. Jahrhundert* (Leipzig, 1928), A. Deichert, 95 pp.

This work presents an account of the nationalist theories of Lagarde, and is particularly useful in relating them to the other religious, philosophical and political currents of nineteenth-century Germany.

204. SEILLIÈRE, ERNEST, *Houston Stewart Chamberlain, le plus récent philosophe du pangermanisme mystique* (Paris, 1917), La Renaissance du livre, 182 pp.

An exposition of the racialist pan-Germanism of H. S. Chamberlain, his borrowings from Rousseau, Kant, Schopenhauer, Gobineau, Nietzsche and Wagner, and his influence on Emperor William II.

205. TOWNSEND, MARY EVELYN, *Origins of Modern German Colonialism, 1871–1885* (New York, 1921), Columbia University Press, 338 pp. "Studies in History, Economics and Public Law," No. 223.

A study of the beginnings of German colonial expansion as a manifestation and expansion of German national patriotism. The book takes up both colonial theories and the actual administrative and political working. The nationalist aspects of the problem are brought out more fully here than in the author's subsequent *Rise and Fall of Germany's Colonial Empire, 1884–1918* (New York, 1930).

206. WERTHEIMER, M. S., *The Pan German League, 1890–1914* (New York, 1924), Columbia University Press, 256 pp. "Studies in History, Economics and Public Law," No. 251.

The Pan German League, or the Alldeutscher Verband, is "an example par excellence of an organization founded to agitate for extreme nationalism." It is, with the Action française, probably the best known of the jingoistic societies. Its importance was exaggerated outside of Germany and on the other hand was minimized considerably within Germany. The author presents a moderate and sane appraisal of the work and activity of the league, the social and economic classes which made up the membership, its organization, ideals and aims, and its activities in foreign lands, its foreign policy and, above all, its influence on governmental policy.

207. KOSOK, PAUL, *Modern Germany. A Study of Conflicting Loyalties* (Chicago, 1933), University of Chicago Press, xxi, 348 pp.

One of the volumes in the series of "Studies in the Making of Citizens," edited by Charles E. Merriam. Although more generally concerned with the social and economic stratification of postwar Germany and the conflicting class loyalties of the various groups, the student of nationalism will find valuable material in Ch. X on the schools, Ch. XIII on localism and sectionalism, Ch. XIV on the relation of Germans to the non-German minorities, and Ch. XVI, by Isidor Ginsburg, on the historical development and psychological significance of national symbols. The work, written before the advent of the Hitler government is nevertheless very useful for the background of the later events.

See also Salz, Arthur, "Nationalismus und Sozialismus im heutigen Deutschland," in *Archiv für Politik und Geschichte*, IV (1925), 290–312.

207a. Snyder, Louis L., *From Bismarck to Hitler. The Background of Modern German Nationalism* (Williamsport, 1935), Bayard Press, xiv, 164 pp.

Studies of Bismarck, Stoecker, Treitschke, Nietzsche, Wagner, William II, Bernhardi and Hitler.

208. KAWERAU, SIEGFRIED, *Denkschrift über die deutschen Geschichts und Lesebücher vor allem seit 1923* (Berlin, 1927), Hensel, 208 pp.

A study of nationalist tendencies and propaganda in the history textbooks used in German schools.

209. SIEBURG, FRIEDRICH, *Es werde Deutschland* (Frankfurt, 1933), Societäts Verlag, 327 pp.
Written after the Hitler revolt of 1933, this is a defense of German nationalism by a former liberal journalist.

The works on German National Socialism are for the most part partisan propaganda either for or against the movement. The following works represent the most serious attempts at analysis:

210. HOOVER, CALVIN B., *Germany Enters the Third Reich* (New York, 1933), Macmillan, 243 pp.
Chapters V-IX contain good material on the political and psychological aspects and principles of National Socialism. The book is weak in its treatment of the history and development of the movement, and suffers from its exaggeration of the anticapitalistic aspects of the movement.

211. HEIDEN, KONRAD, *Geschichte des National Sozialismus. Die Karriere einer Idee* (Berlin, 1932), Rowohlt, 301 pp.
The best and most comprehensive history of German National Socialism by a Liberal Democrat. It was written before Hitler's advent to power. The author's subsequent book, published after the National Socialist Revolution, is not so good.

212. HEUSS, THEODOR, *Hitler's Weg*, (Stuttgart, 1932), Union Verlag, 171 pp.
This work, by a German liberal and one of the leaders of the *Staatspartei*, represents the best analysis of the ideology and political organization of National Socialism.

The following are the most important theoretical writings by proponents and leading advocates of National Socialism:

213. ROSENBERG, ALFRED, *Das Wesensgefüge des Nationalsozialismus. Grundlagen der deutschen Wiedergeburt* (Munich, 1932), Frz. Eher, 80 pp.
A short formulation of Nazi principles by the leading intellectual of the movement.

214. FEDER, GOTTFRIED, *Der deutsche Staat auf nationaler und sozialer Grundlage. Neue Wege in Staat, Finanz und Wirtschaft*, 5th ed. (Munich, 1932), Frz. Eher, 142 pp.
This work is by the leading economic theoretician of the Nazi party.

215. LAUM, BERNARD, *Die geschlossene Wirtschaft. Soziologische Grundlagung des Autarkieproblems* (Tübingen, 1933), J.C.B. Mohr, xvi, 503 pp.
The most thorough National Socialist study of autarchy or extreme economic nationalism.

216. ROSENBERG, ALFRED, *Der Mythus des 20. Jahrhunderts. Eine Wertung der seelisch-geistigen Gestaltenkämpfe unserer Zeit*, 4th ed. (Munich, 1932), Hohenreichen Verlag, 696 pp.
The most ambitious attempt at a Nazi interpretation of history and the historical process and providing the most detailed exposition of National Socialist ideology. The book was not brought out by the official publishing house of the party, and the party has disclaimed responsibility for some of the statements in the book, particularly those directed against the Catholic Church.
See also Nadler, Josef, "Nation, Staat, Dichtung," in *Corona*, IV (1934), 359–74.

216a. UNGER, ERICH, *Das Schrifttum des Nationalsozialismus, 1919–1934* (Berlin, 1934), Junker und Dünnhaupt, xii, 187 pp.
This is an official bibliographical list of all books, pamphlets and articles of National Socialist writers or those ideologically allied to the movement.

THE NATIONALITY PROBLEM IN THE AUSTRO–HUNGARIAN EMPIRE

See also Nos. 17, 44, 105, 106.

217. AUERBACH, BERTRAND, *Les Races et les nationalités en Autriche–Hongrie,* 2d ed. (Paris, 1917), Félix Alcan, xxvi, 492 pp.
The most authoritative and comprehensive study of the nationalities in the old Hapsburg empire. It is very good on demographic aspects, on the individual national movements, and on the problem of cultural contacts.

218. JÁSZI, OSCAR, *The Dissolution of the Habsburg Monarchy* (Chicago, 1929), University of Chicago Press, xxiv, 488 pp.
One of the volumes in the series, "Studies in the Making of Citizens," edited by Charles E. Merriam. Parts III–VII, pp. 133–457, present the most authoritative recent treatment of the nationalist conflict in the old Austro-Hungarian empire. The author is a leading Hungarian writer on the subject, who himself had worked for a democratic federalist solution of the problem. He holds that in its ultimate result the Hapsburg monarchy came to an end owing to its inability to solve the national problem and he places that chief blame on the ruling classes of Hungary. The treatment is both historical and analytical.

219. SAMASSA, PAUL, *Der Völkerstreit im Hapsburgerstaat* (Leipzig, 1910), Dieterichsche Verlagsbuchhandlung, iv, 181 pp.
The conflict of Slav, Hungarian and German nationalities is described in a popular fashion by a patriotic German-Austrian. It is not intended as a scientific work.

220. GEIST–LANYI, PAULA, *Das Nationalitätenproblem auf dem Reichstag zu Kremsier, 1848–49. Ein Beitrag zur Geschichte der Nationalitäten in Oesterreich* (Munich, 1920), Drei Masken Verlag, 210 pp.
Interesting material is brought together on the attitudes of the various nationalities in Austria-Hungary during the 1848 period, with an introduction on the development of the nationality problem up to 1848.

221. RENNER, KARL, (Synopticus), *Staat und Nation. Zur österreichischen Nationalitätenfrage* (Vienna, 1899), Josef Dietl, 42 pp.
This address of Renner's, delivered on February 9, 1899, represents the first clear exposition of the idea of national autonomy as a constitutional means of solving the nationalities problem.

222. HERRNRITT, RUDOLF HERMANN VON, *Nationalität und Recht, dargestellt nach der österreichischen und ausländischen Gesetzgebung* (Vienna, 1899), Hof-Verlag, x, 148 pp.
Despite its age, it is still one of the most valuable works on the relation of nationality to the political state. It is based chiefly on the consideration of the situation in Austria-Hungary.

223. BERNATZIK, E., *Die Ausgestaltung des Nationalgefühls im 19. Jahrhundert. Rechtsstaat und Kulturstaat* (Hanover, 1912), Helwingsche Verlagsbuchhandlung, 94 pp.
The first essay (pp. 1–45) deals chiefly with the nationality problem in Austria and sets forth a moderate program of autonomy.

224. STEINACKER, WOLFGANG, *Der Begriff der Volkszugehörigkeit und die Praxis der Volkszugehörigkeitsbestimmung im alt österreichischen Nationalitätenrecht.* Institut für Sozialforschung in den Alpenländern of the University of Innsbruck, *Schriften,* IX Folge (Innsbruck, 1932), Universitätsverlag, xiii, 65 pp.
A study of the methods of determining nationality—the subjective and objective tests.

225. VINCENTY, CHARLES, *Les Nationalités en Hongrie*, 3d ed. (Geneva, 1918), Édition Atar, 222 pp.
The conflict of nationalities in Hungary is described by a liberal follower of the policy of Déak, emphasizing the primacy of the moral factor. See also No. 54.

226. HEVESEY, ANDRÉ DE, *Nationalities in Hungary*, 2d ed. (London, 1919), T. Fisher Unwin, 247 pp.
A brief survey of the national complexion of Hungary and the various national movements of the nineteenth century, with a plea for the smaller nationalities in Hungary. The author is a follower of the liberal policy of Déak.

NATIONALISM IN THE SLAVIC WORLD

See also Nos. 44, 52, 99, 110, 110a.

For the historical development of nationalism in the Slavic countries, the writings of the following are important: for the *Czechs*, Joseph Dobrowsky, Karl Havlicek, Joseph Jungmann, Jan Kollar, T. G. Massaryk, Franz Palacky and Paul Saffarik; for the *Poles*, Adam Mickiewicz and Hoene-Wronski; for the *Russians*, Peter Chaadayev, Nikolai Danilevsky, Aleksei Homiakov, Nikolai Karamzin, Michail Katkov, Ivan Kireyevsky, Constantin Leontiev, Constantin Pobiednostzoff, Michail Pogodin and Vladimir Soloviev; for the *Ukrainians*, Vladimir Antonovitch, Michail Drahomanov, Ivan Franko, Nikolai Kostomarov, Taras Shevtchenko and Michail Hrusevsky; for the *Serbs and Croats*, Jovan Civijic, Liudewit Gai, Vuk Karadzic, Janez Krek, Juri Krizanic, Dositey Obradovic, Vasa Pelagic, Juray Strossmayer, F. Racki and Jovan Skerlic; for the *Bulgarians*, Hristo Botev, Lubin Karaveloff, Paissi and Georg Venelin; for the *Rumanians*, Georg Lazar, Michael Kogalniceaunu, Alexander Xenopol and N. Jorga; for the *Greeks*, Adamantios Koraes and Constantin Rhigas.

227. FISCHEL, ALFRED, *Der Panslawismus bis zum Weltkriege. Ein geschichtlicher Überblick* (Stuttgart, 1919), J. G. Cotta, vii, 590 pp.
This work, strongly pro-German in tone, is the most comprehensive survey of the nationalist currents in Slavic Europe. The author's general aim is to show pan-Slavism as one of the important causes of the World War. He traces the strong German influence of August Ludwig von Schlözer and Herder on the beginnings of Slavic national movements, and describes the Russians and the Poles as the bearers of the ideal of the political union of the Slavs, and the Slovaks as the bearers of the cultural ideal.
See also Mirtschuk, I., "Der Messianismus bei den Slawen," in *Jahrbücher für Kultur und Geschichte der Slawen*, VI (1930), 223–38.

228. DENIS, ERNEST, *La Bohème depuis la Montagne-Blanche*, 2 vols. (Paris, 1903), Ernest Leroux, 644 and 675 pp.
Volume II presents a thorough account of the Czech renaissance and national movement in the nineteenth century, its relations to other Slav movements and its political and cultural place in Austria-Hungary. The author is the leading French authority on Bohemia.
See also Herben, Jan, "Karl Havlicek, 1821–1856," in *Slavonic Review*, III (1924), 285–303.

229. HASSINGER, HUGO, *Die Entwicklung des tschechischen Nationalbewusstseins und die Gründung des heutigen Staates der Tschechoslawakei* (Kassel, 1928), Johannes Stauda Verlag, 30 pp.

A geographical interpretation of the Czech nationalist movement. The author holds that "as a result of the surrounding of the Czech land by Germans they were constantly driven to the offensive."

230. FISCHEL, ALFRED, *Das tschechische Volk*, 2 vols. (Breslau, 1928), Priebatsch, xvi, 234 pp. and 108 pp.
Volume II contains an essay on Czech national literature, an attempt at an analysis of the national psychology of the Czechs, and a brief discussion of Czech nationalism.

231. MURKO, MATHIAS, *Deutsche Einflüsse auf die Anfänge der böhmischen Romantik* (Graz, 1897), Styria Verlag, xii, 373 pp.
A study of the influence of German Romanticism on the Czech renaissance. Particular attention is given to Palacky, Safarik and Kollar.
See also Oncken, Herman, "Deutsche geistige Einflüsse in der europäischen Nationalbewegung des neunzehnten Jahrhunderts," in *Deutsche Vierteljahrsschrift für Literaturwissenschaft und Geistesgeschichte*, VII (1929), 607–27; Pfitzner, J., "Heinrich Luden und Frantisek Palacky," in *Historische Zeitschrift*, CXLI (1930), 54–96.

232. LEMBERG, EUGEN, *Grundlagen des nationalen Erwachens in Böhmen. Geitesgeschichtliche Studie am Lebensgang Josef Georg Meinerts (1773–1844),* "Veröffentlichungen der slawistischen Arbeitsgemeinschaft an der deutschen Universität in Prag," Reihe I, Heft X (Reichenberg, 1932), Stiepel, 181 pp.
This study is concerned with the influence of Herder and German Romanticism on the beginnings of Slavic national movements, as revealed in the life and literary activity of the Prague journalist and professor Georg Meinert (1773-1844).

233. RADL, EMANUEL, *Der Kampf zwischen Tschechen und Deutschen*, tr. from the Czech by Richard Brandeis (Reichenberg, 1928), Stiepel, 208 pp.
This work, by a leading Czech philosopher, is marked by an honest effort at objectivity and truth. It is valuable for the theoretical discussions of such problems as democracy and nationalism, and the general concept of nationalism. The author's standpoint is to make Czechoslovakia a multinational state of three nationalities (Czech, German, and Hungarian). He makes a sharp attack on the "Czechization" attempts directed at the Germans, and presents a good historical account of Czecho-German relations since earliest times.

234. MOLISCH, PAUL, *Vom Kampf der Tschechen um ihren Staat* (Vienna, 1929), Wilhelm Braumüller, viii, 164 pp.
This work is valuable for its inclusion of much inaccessible material, and presents the story of the Czech movement in Austria from the Austrian side.

235. DENIS, ERNEST, *La Question d'Autriche. Les Slovaques* (Paris, 1917), Librairie Delagrave, 283 pp.
Although war propaganda, this book contains some good material on the Slovak national movement of the nineteenth century.

236. LOCHER, PH. J. G., *Die nationale Differenzierung und Integrierung der Slowaken und Tschechen in ihrem geschichtlichen Verlauf bis 1848* (Haarlem, 1931), Willing, x, 208 pp.
An interpretation of Slovak nationalism as distinguished from the Czech, and a plea for its elevation to actual equality of rank in the Czecho-Slovak state.
See also Prazak, Albert, "The Slavonic Congress of 1848 and the Slovaks," in the *Slavonic Review*, VII (1928), 141–59.

237. FELDMAN, W., *Geschichte der politischen Ideen in Polen seit dessen Teilungen (1795–1914)* (Munich, 1917), R. Oldenbourg, xii, 448 pp.
This book has a decidedly propagandist aim and is a war book. To the non-Polish reader, however, it is useful for revealing the lines of political thought in Poland and the conflicting problems of Polish nationalism during the nineteenth century.
See also Kühne, Walter, "Von den Entwicklung des polnischen Nationalgefühls," in *Volk und Reich*, IX (1933), 623–37; Lednicki, W., "Poland and the Slavophil Idea," in the *Slavonic Review*, VII (1928–29), 128–40, 649–62; Dyboski, Roman, "Literature and National Life in Modern Poland," in the *Slavonic Review*, III (1924), 117–30.

238. GARDNER, MONICA M., *Adam Mickiewicz, the National Poet of Poland* (London, 1911), J. M. Dent, xv, 317 pp.
This is a eulogistic literary biography, and not a study of nationalism. It is of some value, in view of the lack of material in English.
See also Kallenbach, J., and others, on Adam Mickiewicz in the *Monde Slave*, n.s. VI (1932), 321–496.

239. GARDNER, MONICA M., *Kościuszko, a Biography* (London, 1920), Allen and Unwin, 211 pp.
An enthusiastic account of the famous Polish patriot and his uprising.

240. MASSARYK, THOMAS G., *The Spirit of Russia. Studies in History, Literature and Philosophy*, tr. from the German by Eden and Cedar Paul, 2 vols. (London, 1919), Allen and Unwin, xxii, 480 pp. and xix, 585 pp.
These volumes present a mine of information on Russian Slavophilism and Panslavism. There are also brief sections, in the first volume, on Panslavism among the Czechs, Slovaks, Poles and Southern Slavs.

241. KOYRÉ, ALEXANDRE, *La Philosophie et le problème national en Russie au debut du xixe siècle* (Paris, 1929), Champion, 212 pp. "Bibliothèque de l'Institut française de Leningrad," Vol. X.
The author traces the influence of German idealistic philosophy on the early development of Slavophilism.
See also Shmurlo, E., "From Krizanic to the Slavophils," in *Slavonic Review*, VI (1927), 320–35; Koyré, A., "Russia's Place in the World. Peter Chaadayev and the Slavophils," in the *Slavonic Review*, V (1927), 594–608 (this is an English translation of part of Koyré's above-mentioned book); Stojanvic, J. D., "The First Slavophils: Homyakov and Kireyevsky," in the *Slavonic Review*, VI (1928), 561–78; Lanz, Henry, "The Philosophy of Kirievsky," in the *Slavonic Review*, IV (1926), 594–604. For the Ukrainian movement, see Dorosenko, D., "Die Entwicklung der ukrainischen Geschichtsidee vom Ende des 18. Jahrhunderts bis zur Gegenwart," in *Jahrbücher für Kultur und Geschichte der Slawen*, IV (1928), 363–79.

241a. TIANDER, KARL, *Das Erwachen Osteuropas. Die Nationalitätenbewegung in Russland und der Weltkrieg* (Vienna, 1934), Wilhelm Braumüller, viii, 184 pp.
An attempt at a history of the national movements in Russia, up to the Bolshevist revolution.

242. HECKER, J. F., *Russian Sociology* (New York, 1915), Columbia University Press, 311 pp.
While not primarily a work on nationalism, this is useful, as one of the few works available in English, for an intelligent discussion of the Slavophils and Westernists.

243. MILIUKOV, PAUL, *Le Mouvement intellectuel russe*, tr. from the Russian by J. W. Bienstock (Paris, 1918), Éditions Bossard, 449 pp.
This famous work of Miliukov's contains an excellent essay on the Slav-

ophile doctrines of Danilevski, Leontiev and Vladimir Soloviev (pp. 377–439).

244. KOHN, HANS, *Nationalism in the Soviet Union*, tr. from the German (New York, 1933), Columbia University Press, xi, 164 pp.

The author views the problem as that of a conflict of two theologies, nationalism and communism, or supranationalism. He gives an account of the views of Lenin and Stalin on the nationalities question, and the evolution of the Soviet system of a supranational state which grants linguistic freedom and right of self-government to all the 185 nationalities comprising the Soviet Union, but which seeks to replace the national cultures of these peoples, rooted in historical bourgeois tradition, by a new supranational faith of communism.

See also Cleinow, Georg, "Die Grundgedanken der Nationalitätenpolitik in der Sowjetunion," in *Osteuropa*, I (1925–26), 65–73, 129–44; Dobranitzki, M., "Die Nationalitätenpolitik der Sowjet-Union," in *Europäische Gespräche*, IV (1926), 230–54; Biehahn, W., "Marxismus und nationale Idee in Russland," in *Osteuropa*, IX (1934), 461–76. See also Nos. 110, 110a.

245. YARMOLINSKY, AVRAHM, *The Jews and Other Minor Nationalities under the Soviets* (New York, 1928), Vanguard Press, xiv, 193 pp.

While chiefly concerned with the new position of the Jew in Soviet Russia and the attempts to change his place in society, the second part of the book (pp. 141–86) recounts briefly the nationalities policy of the Soviet Union and gives a table of the different peoples found in the Soviet Union.

246. HARPER, SAMUEL NORTHRUP, *Civic Training in Soviet Russia* (Chicago, 1929), University of Chicago Press, xvii, 401 pp.

One of the volumes in the series, "Studies in the Making of Citizens," edited by Charles Merriam. Ch. XVI, pp. 343–66, deals with the problem of nationalism and internationalism in the Soviet Union.

247. TOBIEN, ALEXANDER VON, *Die livländische Ritterschaft in ihrem Verhältnis zum Zarismus und russischen Nationalismus*, 2 vols. Vol. I, (Riga, 1925), G. Löffler, xv, 523 pp; Vol. II (Berlin, 1930), Walter de Gruyter, xviii, 412 pp.

A very detailed and authoritative account of the attempts at Russification in Latvia in church, schools and public administration, and a history of the rise and development of the Latvian national movement, to the creation of an independent Latvia and the resulting changes, especially along agrarian lines.

248. SETON-WATSON, ROBERT WILLIAM, *The Rise of Nationality in the Balkans* (London, 1917), Constable, viii, 308 pp.

A review of the eastern question down to eve of the Treaty of Bucharest, August, 1913. The author is the leading champion of the Southern Slavs in Great Britain. The work is chiefly concerned with political developments.

See also Ivanov, Yordan, "Le Peuple Bulgare et ses manifestations nationales et morales," in *Comité national d'études sociales et politiques, Rapports et Conferences* (1921), 32 pp.

249. GEWEHR, WESLEY MARSH, *The Rise of Nationalism in the Balkans, 1800–1930* (New York, 1931), Henry Holt, xi, 137 pp.

A brief outline, mainly on the evolution of the independent political states in the Balkans.

250. MURRAY, WILLIAM SMITH, *The Making of the Balkan States* (New York, 1910), Columbia University Press, 199 pp. "Studies in History, Economics and Public Law," No. 102.

The author discusses the relations of the Balkan states to Turkey and to Russia, the attitude of the Great Powers, and the diplomatic history of the attainment of independence by Serbia, Montenegro, Greece and Rumania.

251. PASVOLSKY, LEO, *Economic Nationalism of the Danubian States* (New York, 1928), Macmillan, xviii, 609 pp.

A detailed study of the economic results of the national dismemberment of Austria-Hungary, the national economic policies of each of the succession states, and the problem of a Danubian economic or customs union.

252. WENDEL, HERMANN, *Der Kampf der Südslawen um Freiheit und Einheit* (Frankfurt, 1925), Frankfurter Societäts-Druckerei, 798 pp.

This is the most comprehensive account of the nationalist movement of the Southern Slavs from the first Serbian revolt to the erection of the Jugo-Slav state. The cultural renaissance, as well as political movements, are dealt with adequately. The author is an enthusiastic but uncritical admirer of the Southern Slavs as against their oppressors.

See also Civijic, Jovan, "Studies in Jugoslav Psychology," in the *Slavonic Review*, IX (1930–31), 375–90, 662–81, and X (1931), 58–79; Matl, Joseph, "Die Entstehung des jugoslavischen Staates," in *Zeitschrift für Politik*, XVI (1926), 521–43, and "Materialien zur Entstehungsgeschichte des südslawischen Staates," in *Jahrbücher für Kultur und Geschichte der Slawen*, II (1926), 53–80; Wendel, Hermann, "Marxism and the Southern Slavs," in the *Slavonic Review*, II (1923), 289–307.

253. WENDEL, HERMANN, *Aus dem südslawischen Risorgimento* (Gotha, 1921), Friedrich Andreas Perthes, v, 199 pp.

Biographical sketches of the Southern Slav nationalist leaders: Dositey Obradovic, pp. 1–30; Ljudevit Gai, pp. 31–72; the Omladina, pp. 73–102; Josip Juroj Strossmayer, pp. 103–34; Svetozar Markovic, pp. 137–66; Janez Krek, pp. 167–94.

See also Loiseau, Charles, "La Politique de Strossmayer," in *Monde Slave*, n. s., IV, Part I (1927), 379–405; and "Un Précurseur de l'unité Yougoslave: Mgr. Strossmayer," in *Vie des peuples*, IX (1923), 941–57; Lalic, N., "Les Idées de Strossmayer," in *Monde Slave*, n. s., VI, Part IV (1929), 442–49.

254. LAURIAN, MARIUS A., *Le Principe des nationalités et l'unité nationale roumaine* (Paris, 1923), Jouve et Cie., 102 pp.

A study of Rumanian nationalism concerned chiefly with demonstrating the historical rights of Rumania to Transylvania, the Banat, Bukowina, Bessarabia and the Dobrudja.

See also No. 372.

NATIONALISM IN FRANCE

See also Nos. 4, 18, 47, 66, 99, 111, 112, 113, 114, 140.

For the historical development of French nationalism, the writings of the following are important: the anthropological writings of Henri Boulainvilliers, Joseph Arthur de Gobineau, Julien Joseph Virey and Vacher de Lapouge; the litterateurs, Maurice Barrès, Léon Bloy, Paul Déroulède, Victor Hugo, Alphonse de Lamartine, Charles Maurras, Charles Péguy, Mme. de Staël and Hippolyte Taine; the political theorists, Louis Gabriel de Bonald, François Chateaubriand, Joseph de Maistre, Napoleon III, Ernest Renan, Abbe de Sieyès and Louis Adolphe Thiers; the historians, Fustel de Coulanges, Henri Martin, Jules Michelet and Augustin Thierry.

255. SIEGFRIED, ANDRÉ, *France, a Study in Nationality* (New Haven, 1930), Yale University Press, vi, 122 pp.
Prefaced to a brilliant study of French politics is a provocative discussion of French national character (Chs. I–II).

256. SIEBURG, FRIEDRICH, *Who Are These French?* translated from the German by Allan Harris (New York, 1932), Macmillan, 303 pp.
A brilliant study of French national character and also of the national mission idea in France, by a German journalist who has an intimate acquaintance with the land. The American edition also includes a letter to the author by Bernard Grasset, taken from the French edition, and a reply by the author.

257. BRUNHES, JEAN, *Géographie humaine de la France*, Vols. I and II of *Histoire de la nation française*, edited by Gabriel Hanotaux, 15 vols. (Paris, 1920–29), Librairie Plon.
Volume I, Ch. III, pp. 105–50, is a discussion of the racial composition of France and the formation of a unified nation out of a diversity of races.

258. BARZUN, JACQUES, *The French Race* (New York, 1932), Columbia University Press, 275 pp. "Studies in History, Economics and Public Law," No. 375.
This book treats of the origins of the French race as seen by Tacitus and Cæsar; of the actual mixture of the races as seen by modern scholars, and the political forces that ushered in and perpetuated race theorizing from the sixteenth century on. It presents a good account of the theories of the origins of French culture and institutions. Among the most important theorists considered are Gregory of Tours, Pasquier, Hotman, Mezeray, Fénelon, Boulainvilliers, Fréret, Dubos, Montesquieu, Mably and Sieyès. The book is particularly valuable in showing how this theorizing was used to defend or to attack particular social and political ideas and institutions, and how the controversy, revived in more acute form by the work of Gobineau, is still a living factor in French life and scholarship. It is significant as a history of French ideas as well as for the study of one of the great myths of nationalism, the race myth.

259. BENDA, JULIEN, *Esquisse d'une histoire des Français dans leur volonté d'être une nation* (Paris, 1932), Gallimard, 273 pp.
The author holds that the French nation was formed, not by kings or governments, but by the will of France itself. This is revealed chiefly in questions of territorial unity and central authority. This work is a philosophical interpretation of the formation of the French nation, in which the rationalist author of *The Treason of the Intellectuals* betrays a good deal of Jacobin nationalism.
Cf. the review by Emmanuel Berl in *Europe*, XXX (1932), 272–75.

260. MARTIN-SAINT-LÉON, Et., *Les Sociétés de la nation. Étude sur les éléments constitutifs de la nation française* (Paris, 1930), Édition Spès, 415 pp.
In Ch. IV, pp. 94–118, the author analyzes the racial composition of the French people and presents an attempt at a psychological study of the national characteristics of the regions and of the French as a whole.

261. BRUNOT, FERDINAND, *Histoire de la langue française des origines à 1900* Vols. I–IX (Paris, 1924–33), Armand Colin.
Vol. VII, 360 pp., deals with the propagation of the French language within France up to the revolution, and Vol. IX, Part I, 616 pp., covers in great detail the emergence of French as the national language under the Revolution and the Empire in education, public life and the Church. See also Febvre, Lucien, "Langue et nationalité en France au xviiie siècle," in the *Revue de synthése historique*, XLII (1926), 19–40.

262. GROSJEAN, GEORGES, *Le Sentiment national dans la Guerre de Cent Ans* (Paris, 1928), Édition Bossard, 233 pp.
This is a treatment of patriotic feeling in France during the Hundred Years' War and is directed against the thesis that there was no nationalism in France before the Revolution. It is more popular than scientific, and concerned more with patriotism than with nationalism. Joan of Arc is pictured as the great national heroine.

263. AULARD, A., *Le Patriotisme français de la Renaissance à la Révolution* (Paris, 1921), Chiron, 283 pp.
This is a war book, based on lectures delivered in 1914–16. It is motivated by a desire to show that French patriotism is reasonable, philosophic, and inspired by love of liberty and humanity. It traces French patriotism in Voltaire, Rousseau, d'Alembert, Jaucourt, Turgot, Louis XVI and the cahiers of 1789 up to the great federation 1790, when France really became a *patrie*. The greater part of the book deals with the Revolutionary period.
Cf. Kruscewski, W., "Der französische Nationsbegriff," in *Nation und Staat*, III (1929–30), 149–57.

264. HAYMANN, FRANZ, *Weltbürgertum und Vaterlandsliebe in der Staatslehre Rousseaus and Fichtes* (Berlin, 1924), Rudolf Heise, 110 pp.
The chief object of this study is to show that Rousseau's political philosophy was not purely cosmopolitan and that Fichte's not purely nationalistic. Rousseau's nationalism was pragmatic and utilitarian, while Fichte looked upon the nation as the bearer of an ethical idea.

264a. Cobban, Alfred, *Rousseau and the Modern State* (London, 1934), Allen and Unwin, 288 pp.
Ch. VI, pp. 151–91, contains a good discussion of Rousseau and the nation state.

265. HOFFMANN-LINKE, EVA, *Zwischen Nationalismus und Demokratie. Gestalten der französischen Vorrevolution* (Munich, 1927), R. Oldenbourg, vii, 313 pp. *Historische Zeitschrift*, Beiheft IX.
The thesis of this book is that 1789 did not bring about "a nation," but that nationalism existed before. The author confuses the terms nationalism and democracy, which she sets up as contradictory. The book is very weak on the general pre-Revolutionary social and economic history. The best part is the analysis of cosmopolitan and nationalist ideas in the individual thinkers—Montesquieu, Voltaire, Rousseau, the encyclopædists, Condorcet and Mirabeau.

266. HYSLOP, BEATRICE FRY, *French Nationalism in 1789 according to the General Cahiers* (New York, 1934), Columbia University Press, xix, 343 pp.
A very careful study of nationality, democracy, *étatisme*, patriotism and nationalism as reflected in the general cahiers of 1789. The book is particularly valuable for its factual and statistical analysis.

267. BRINTON, CRANE, *The Jacobins. An Essay in the New History* (New York, 1930), Macmillan, x, 319 pp.
The nationalist elements of Jacobinism and how it turned from cosmopolitanism to French nationalism are touched on in Ch. V; the patriotic ritual and cults are treated in Ch. VI.
See also Gershoy, Leo, "Barère, Champion of Nationalism in the French Revolution," in the *Political Science Quarterly*, XLII (1927), 419–30.

268. VAN DEUSEN, GLYNDON G., *Sieyès: His Life and Nationalism* (New York, 1932), Columbia University Press, 170 pp. "Studies in History, Economics and Public Law," No. 362.
Chapters V–VIII deal with his nationalist doctrines, his rôle in the territorial reorganization of France and his nationalistic foreign policy.

269. MATHIEZ, ALBERT, *Les Origines des cultes revolutionnaires, 1789–1792* (Paris, 1904), Société nouvelle, 151 pp.
A study of the religion of patriotism in the French Revolution, with its cults, symbols and ceremonial practices, and its conflict with Christianity.

270. WALSH, HENRY H., *The Concordat of 1801. A Study of the Problem of Nationalism in the Relations of Church and State* (New York, 1933), Columbia University Press, 259 pp. "Studies in History, Economics and Public Law," No. 387.
A study of the clash between French nationalism and the internationalism of the Catholic Church, its effect on the Concordat of 1801, and the nationalist theorizing by leading French churchmen and politicians of the time, who considered the problem of church and state. Those discussed at greater length are Chateaubriand, Jean-Etienne-Marie Portalis, Jean Siffrein Maury, Henri Gregoire, Jacques-Andre Emery, Paul-Therese-David d'Astros and Joseph de Maistre.

271. ROHDEN, PETER RICHARD, *Joseph de Maistre als politischer Theoretiker* (Munich, 1929), Verlag der Münchner Drucke, 280 pp. "Forschungen zur mittelalterlichen und neueren Geschichte," Vol. II.
An excellent analysis of the traditionalism of de Maistre.

272. STEWART, HUGH FRASER, and PAUL DESJARDINS, *French Patriotism in the Nineteenth Century Traced in Contemporary Texts* (Cambridge, 1923), Cambridge University Press, xliv, 333 pp.
One hundred and sixteen extracts from the writings of French patriots from 1792 to 1830, in the original French, with an introductory essay in English on the origins of French nationalism.

273. PLATZ, HERMANN, *Geistige Kämpfe in modernen Frankreich* (Munich, 1922), Kösel and Pustet, xix, 672 pp.
These essays, written from a Catholic standpoint, present an intimate account of a cross section of intellectual currents in modern France and their interaction with nationalism and religious doctrines. It includes extended treatments of Taine and French nationalism, the political nationalism of Barrès and Maurras, the literary nationalism of the Neo-Classicists, and the struggle between nationalist and internationalist currents. The author views all these movements as a return to traditionalism.

274. KÜHN, JOACHIM, editor, *Der Nationalismus im Leben der dritten Republik* (Berlin, 1920), Paetel, ix, 373 pp.
All the contributors aim to show the extreme nationalist and warlike spirit of France in each of the fields they cover. The essays included are: (1) Kühn, J., "Der Nationalismus im politischen Leben der dritten Republik," pp. 1–78; (2) Platz, H., "Der Nationalismus im französischen Denken der Vorkriegszeit," pp. 79–126; (3) Gruber, H., "Der Nationalismus in der französischen Freimaurerei," pp. 127–58; (4) Eberz, O., "Die Gallikanische Kirche als Werckzeug der Revanche," pp. 159–79; (5) Ruhlmann, P., "Der Revanche Gedanke in der französischen Schule," pp. 180–206; (6) Windelband, W., "Der Nationalismus in der französischen Geschichtschreibung seit 1871," pp. 207–39; (7) Kuhn, J., and H. Platz, "Der Nationalismus in der französischen Dichtung seit 1871," pp. 240–84; (8) Becker, M. L., "Die französische Volksbühne als Verhetzungsmittel," pp. 285–300; (9) Salm, M., "Der Angriffsgedanke in der französischen Militärliteratur seit 1871," pp. 301–27; (10) Kuhn, J., "Der französische Nationalismus in seiner letzten Phase," pp. 328–73.

275. FRANK, WALTER, *Nationalismus und Demokratie im Frankreich der dritten Republik, 1871 bis 1918* (Hamburg, 1933), Hanseatische Verlagsanstalt, 652 pp.
This is a reflection of extreme German conservative nationalism of the postwar period in the treatment of the history of the French Republic.

It is extremely antidemocratic and much more sympathetic with the integral nationalism of Barrès and Maurras, to which the author devotes a very long section of the book.

276. ISRAEL, ALEXANDRE, *L'École de la république: la grande œuvre de Jules Ferry* (Paris, 1931), Librairie Hachette, x, 273 pp.
The educational activities of one of the most important creators of French national education.

277. HAYES, CARLTON J. H., *France, a Nation of Patriots* (New York, 1930), Columbia University Press, x, 487 pp. "Social and Economic Studies of Post-War France," Vol. V.
A very impartial and objective study of the current manifestations of French nationalism. An analysis of the French national psychology, rooted in the Catholic Church and in centralized government, and a discussion of the inculcation of patriotism by the government, the educational system, the army and navy, church, press, radio and movies, national societies, and symbols and ceremonies. There is a good discussion of French regionalism and also a very valuable appendix on textbooks used in the schools, with a digest of their contents.

278. CURTIUS, ERNST ROBERT, *Maurice Barrès und die geistigen Grundlagen des französischen Nationalismus* (Bonn, 1921), Friedrich Cohen, viii, 255 pp.
This is the best treatment of Barrès and recent French nationalism, by a German literary critic possessed of a most intimate acquaintance with French civilization.
See also Guérard, Albert Leon, "Maurice Barrès and the Doctrine of Nationalism," in the *Texas Review*, I (1916), 275–90.

279. GURIAN, WALDEMAR, *Der integrale Nationalismus in Frankreich. Charles Maurras und die Action française* (Frankfort, 1931), Klostermann Verlag, 131 pp.
The author traces the development of Maurras from the advocate of nihilism and anarchism to the disciple of order and monarchy. He attributes the lack of influence of the Action française to its aristocratic character as a club of doctrinaires and *literati*. The book is one of the best analyses of the doctrines of the Action française, bringing out its universal interest as the oldest antidemocratic and antiparliamentarian movement.
See also Mitchell, M. Marion, "Emile Durkheim and the Philosophy of Nationalism," in the *Political Science Quarterly*, XLVI (1931), 87–106.

280. ROUX, MARIE DE, *Charles Maurras et le nationalisme de l'Action française* (Paris, 1927), Bernard Grasset, 272 pp.
A sympathetic exposition of the doctrines of Maurras, pointing out the differences between his personal doctrines and the general doctrines of the Action française, and their relation to the Catholic Church.

281. MURET, CHARLOTTE T., *French Royalist Doctrine since the Revolution* (New York, 1933), Columbia University Press, viii, 326 pp.
A comprehensive study of royalist doctrines in France, with special attention to Chateaubriand, Royer-Collard, Benjamin Constant, Guizot, the various royal claimants, La Tour du Pin and the Action française.

282. GUY-GRAND, GEORGES, *La Philosophie nationaliste* (Paris, 1911), Bernard Grasset, 223 pp.
A critique of the philosophy of the Action française by a liberal democratic philosopher.

283. CHENU, C., *La Ligue des patriotes* (Paris, 1916), Recueil Sirey, ix, 137 pp.
The program and history of Déroulède's Ligue des Patriotes, by one of its leaders.

284. DUCRAY, CAMILLE, *Paul Déroulède, 1846–1914* (Paris, 1914), Librairie Ambert, xiii, 275 pp.
A biography of the extreme French patriot by an admirer and follower.

285. THARAUD, JÊROME and JEAN, *La Vie et la mort de Déroulède* (Paris, 1925), Plon, 281 pp.
A popular, sympathetic biography.

285a. MOUNIER, EMMANUEL, MARCEL PÉGUY and GEORGES IZARD, *La Pensée de Charles Péguy* (Paris, 1931), Plon, viii, 424 pp.
This volume contains three sympathetic essays on the general thought of Péguy, his political and social views and his Catholicism. The nationalist aspects of his thought are treated only in scattered passages through the volume.

286. BRUN, CHARLES, *Le Régionalisme*, 3d ed. (Paris, 1911), Bloud, 289 pp.
This is the classic treatise on French regionalism by its most distinguished leader.
See also No. 53, and Hintze, Hedwig, "Der französische Regionalismus und seine Wurzeln," in the *Preussische Jahrbücher*, CLXXXI (1920), 347–76.

287. HINTZE, HEDWIG, *Staatseinheit und Föderalismus im alten Frankreich und in der Revolution* (Stuttgart, 1928), Deutsche Verlagsanstalt, xxx, 623 pp.
The author conceives of French history as a struggle between the unitary centralization and federal regionalism, which reached its climax in the revolutionary struggle between the Jacobins and Girondists. The French nation arose from the federations of 1790. This is the most exhaustive treatment of the subject.

288. BERLET, C., *Les Tendances unitaires et provincialistes en France à la fin du xviiie siècle* (Nancy, 1913), Imprimeries Réunies de Nancy, 280 pp.
A study of the influence of nationalism on political and administrative decisions in France; the struggle between national centralizing interests and localism, crowned by the nationalist act of the French Revolution and the National Assembly.

289. DUBREUIL, LÉON, *L'Idée régionaliste sous la Révolution* (Besancon, 1919), Maillot Frères, 123 pp.
A study of public opinion on the question of centralization during the French Revolution. The author aims to show that it was brought about by necessity only, and not because of a desire on the part of the Revolutionary leaders to stifle local autonomy.

290. PARISET, GEORGES, *Études d'histoire révolutionnaire et contemporaine* (Paris, 1929), Société d'édition des Belles Lettres.
Pages 287–313 contain a brief survey of French regionalism from the centralization under the monarchy up to the modern regionalist reaction.

291. GOOCH, R. K., *Regionalism in France* (New York, 1931), Century Co., 129 pp.
This work is mainly concerned with the question of administration, control and decentralization, and is written from a viewpoint favorable to decentralization. It also touches on the nationalist implications of the problem, especially in Ch. VI on "Sentimental Manifestations of Regionalism."

292. BRUN, CHARLES, *Mistral* (Paris, 1930), Éditions du Monde moderne, 84 pp.
A eulogistic appreciation of Mistral and his relation to the regionalist movement.

293. HENNESSY, JEAN, *Régions de France (1911-1916)* (Paris, 1916), Georges Cres, vii, 284 pp.
A collection of articles and addresses by one of the leading champions of economic regionalism in France.

294. JEAN-DESTIEUX, F., *L'Évolution régionaliste: du félibrige au fédéralisme* (Paris, 1918), Bossard, xv, 239 pp.
A regionalist program for France by a prominent regionalist leader. It is based mainly on collections of extracts from other writers.

295. JEAN-DESTIEUX, F., *L'Évolution régionaliste: Produire* (Paris, 1919), Éditions Bossard, 335 pp.
The economic aspects of French regionalism.

296. HAUSER, HENRI, *Le Probléme du régionalisme* (Paris, 1924), Les Presses universitaires, xii, 176 pp.
A detailed study of the effects of the World War on the development of economic regionalism in France up to 1921.

297. PREVET, FRANÇOIS, *Le Régionalisme économique: Conception et réalisation* (Paris, 1929), Recueil Sirey, vi, 295 pp.
A valuable complement to the work of Henri Hauser (No. 296).

298. DUHAMEL, MAURICE, *La Question bretonne dans son cadre européen* (Paris, 1929), André Delpeuch, 238 pp.
A history of the regionalist movement in Brittany and an exposition of its doctrines and relation to French national unity, by a leading exponent of the Breton autonomist movement.

NATIONALISM IN BELGIUM AND THE NETHERLANDS

See also Nos. 54, 82.

299. KURTH, G., *La Nationalité belge* (Namur, 1913), Picard, 213 pp.
The author insists that there is a Belgian nationality, despite the absence of natural frontiers and racial or linguistic unity. What unites the people of Belgium is the "common enjoyment of a régime of liberty and fidelity to the same institutions." He attributes the progressive development of Belgian nationality to Brabant, and considers Flanders as the home of provincial particularism.
See also Grosse, F., "Die belgische Nationalitätenfrage," in the *Europäische Revue*, X (1934), 348-52.

300. CLOUGH, SHEPARD BANCROFT, *A History of the Flemish Movement in Belgium; A Study in Nationalism.* (New York, 1930), Richard R. Smith, vii, 316 pp.
This is the most complete work on the Flemish nationalist movement, tracing it from its origins up to present day, and taking up all the linguistic, cultural, economic, political administrative and international aspects.

301. HAMÉLIUS, P., *Historie politique et littéraire du mouvement flamand au xixe siècle*, 2d ed. (Brussels, 1924), L'Eglantine, 335 pp.
This is the best French study of the Flemish movement, giving most attention to the question of language and cultural movements.
See also Leemans, Victor, "Zur Soziologie des flämischen Nationalismus," in the *Europäische Revue*, X (1934), 344-47.

302. DAUMONT, F., *Le Mouvement flamand*, 2 vols. (Brussels, 1911), Société Belge de Librairie, ix, 377 and 335 pp.
A detailed survey of linguistic, social, economic and educational aspects of the Flemish problem, but very partial and often inaccurate.

303. BÄHRENS, KURT, *Flanderns Kampf um die eigene Scholle. Eine Studie seiner wirtschaftlichen Struktur* (Breslau, 1930), K. Vater, 204 pp.

A brief summary of the nineteenth-century Flemish movement, with the chief emphasis on the development of an independent Flemish economy. It is very favorably disposd to the Flemings.

304. DESTRÉE, JULES, *Wallons et Flamands, la querelle linguistique* (Paris, 1923), Plon, 187 pp.

The Walloon-Flemish problem is treated by a prominent Walloon Socialist leader, who denies the existence of a Belgian nationality and advocates the recognition of Belgium as a binational state, with administrative autonomy for each nationality.

See also Vandervelde, E., "Belgian Foreign Policy and the Nationalities Question," in *Foreign Affairs*, XI (1933), 657–70.

305. FOULON, F., *La Question wallone* (Brussels, 1918), A. Leempoel, xi, 203 pp.

The dual-nationalism problem in Belgium by an enthusiastic Walloon, strongly anti-Flemish.

306. HUIZINGA, J., *Wege der Kulturgeschichte*, translated from the Dutch by Werner Kaegi (Munich, 1930), Drei Masken Verlag, 405 pp.

The essay "Aus der Vorgeschichte des niederlandischen Nationalbewusstseins," pp. 208–80, is a masterly study of the conditions and factors in the early modern period which brought about the differentiation of Holland from what is now Belgium. The main factor was not ethnic nor economic, but rather the political policy of Burgundy.

See also No. 54, and Geyl, P., "Einheit and Entzweiung in den Niederlanden," in the *Historische Zeitschrift*, CXXXIX (1929), 48–61.

NATIONALISM IN THE SCANDINAVIAN COUNTRIES

For the historical development of nationalism in Norway, the writings of the following are important: Björnson, Keyser, Peter Andreas Munk, J. E. Sars, Welhaven and Hendrik Wergeland; for Sweden: Lorenzp Hammarsköld, Per Daniel Atterbom, Vilhelm F. Parmblad, Erik Geijer, Essaias Tegnér and Anders Fryxell; for Denmark: Holberg and Grundtvig; for Finland: Ivor Aasen, Adolf Arwidson, Johann Runeberg, Johann V. Snellmann and G. Z. Yrjö-Koskinen.

307. ELVIKEN, ANDREAS, *Die Entwicklung des norwegischen Nationalismus* (Berlin, 1930), E. Ebering, 132 pp. "Historische Studien," No. CXCVIII.

An interpretation of the rise of Norwegian nationalism down to the beginnings of the *landsmal* movement. The author attacks the thesis of Halvdan Koht that Norwegian nationalism is the product of the class struggle of the peasantry. He presents it as a product of the opposition between urban and agricultural population, peasantry and Danish officialdom, pietistic popular Christianity and the Danish state official church, and traces the influence of Montesquieu, Voltaire, the Physiocrats and the German Romanticists. Particular attention is given to Wergeland, Welhaven, Keyser and Munch. A portion of this book was published in the *Journal of Modern History*, III (1931), 365–91. Cf. No. 309.

308. FALNES, OSCAR JULIUS, *National Romanticism in Norway* (New York, 1933), Columbia University Press, 399 pp. "Studies in History, Economics and Public Law," No. 386.

This is the most detailed study of Norwegian nationalism, with particular reference to the intellectual influences of Romanticism as revealed in the works of historians, folklorists and philologists.

309. KOHT, HALVDAN, *Les Luttes des paysans de Norvège du xvie au xixe siècle*, translated from the Norwegian by E. Guerre (Paris, 1929), Payot, 315 pp.
An interpretation of the rise of Norwegian nationalism in terms of the class struggle, particularly as the result of the peasant movements. Cf. No. 307.

310. BENSON, A. B., *The Old Norse Element in Swedish Romanticism* (New York, 1914), Columbia University Press, xii, 193 pp.
This work reveals a phenomenon common to all national movements — the return to a heroic past. In Sweden this was the work of the Fosforists and the Gothic school, who brought back into the consciousness of the Swedish intellectual classes the life, customs and the literature of the old Norse elements. The author also traces the interacting influence of German authors like Herder, Tieck and Novalis.

311. BEGTRUP, HOLGER, HANS LUND, and PETER MANNICHE, *The Folk High Schools of Denmark and the Development of a Farming Community*, new ed. (London, 1929), Oxford University Press, 176 pp.
Book II, by Holger Begtrup, is on the history of the folk high schools and contains an account of the life and work of N. F. S. Grundtvig. This is the most important section of the book for the problem of Danish nationalism.

312. CAMPBELL, OLIVE DAME, *The Danish Folk School. Its Influence in the Life of Denmark and the North* (New York, 1928), Macmillan, xvi, 359 pp.
Contains a few pages on the nationalist ideas of Bishop Grundtvig. See also Paul-Dubois, L., "Grundtvig et le relèvement du Danemark au xixe siècle," in the *Revue des deux mondes*, 5th series, LII (1909), 656–76.

313. WUORINEN, J. H., *Nationalism in Modern Finland* (New York, 1931), Columbia University Press, x, 302 pp.
This is not only a history of the nationalist movement, but a history of Finland in the nineteenth century, in which the national question is all dominant. The author shows that nationalism in Finland did not begin until the separation from Sweden in 1808–9, and that it arose from the apprehension that Finland might be absorbed into the Russian empire. He discusses the peculiar problem of the bilingual character of the nation, and the struggle between the Finn and the Swede-Finn, the contributions of the scholars and the literary men, the studies in history and folklore and national literature, and carries the story down to the postwar period and the creation of an independent Finland.
See also No. 52.

NATIONALISM IN SWITZERLAND

See also Nos. 44, 48.

314. DUMUR, LOUIS, *Les deux Suisse, 1914–1917* (Paris, 1917), Éditions Bossard, 320 pp.
A war book by a strong Pro-French Swiss journalist, but interesting in revealing the divergence of national feeling within Switzerland during the World War.

315. WEILENMANN, HERMANN, *Die vielsprachige Schweiz. Eine Lösung des Nationalitäten-problems* (Basle, 1925), Im Rhein Verlag, 301 pp.

A historical study of the solution of the language problem in the multilingual Switzerland.

316. BROOKS, ROBERT CLARKSON, *Civic Training in Switzerland. A Study of Democratic Life* (Chicago, 1930), University of Chicago Press, xxi, 436 pp.
A volume in the series, "Studies in the Making of Citizens" edited by Charles Merriam. The author is concerned chiefly with Switzerland as a political state, rather than with the problem of nationality or the conflict of nationalities in the multilingual Switzerland. Some interesting pages related to the subject of Swiss nationalism are found, however, in Ch. X on patriotic societies, Ch. XII on national symbolism, and Ch. XV on traditionalism and local patriotism.

NATIONALISM IN ITALY

See also Nos. 99, 112, 138.

For the historical development of Italian nationalism, the writings of the following are important: Vittorio Alfieri, Cesare Balbo, Carlo Botta, Giosuè Carducci, Enrico Corradini, Vincenzo Cuoco, Massimo D'Azeglio, Giuseppe Ferrari, Ugo Foscolo, Vincenzo Gioberti, Giaccomo Leopardi, Niccolo Machiavelli, Pasquale Mancini, Giuseppe Mazzini, Vincenzo Monti, Benito Mussolini, Pellegrino Rossi, Bertranò and Silvio Spaventa, and Niccolo Tommaseo.

317. KING, BOLTON, *A History of Italian Unity*, 2 vols. (London, 1899), Nisbet, x, 416 pp. and 451 pp.
While chiefly a political history of the Risorgimento, this work also deals in detail with the cultural and social aspects of the various shades of the nationalist movement of 1814–71. It is a standard work on the subject.

318. THAYER, WILLIAM ROSCOE, *The Dawn of Italian Independence*, 2 vols. (Boston, 1892), Houghton Mifflin, 453 pp. and 446 pp.
This is primarily a political history of Italy from 1814 to 1849. It deals only with the external aspects of the Italian national movement.

319. BOURGIN, GEORGES, *La Formation de l'unité italienne* (Paris, 1929), Armand Colin, 220 pp.
A popular survey of Italian unification from the eighteenth century to 1919. The author stresses chiefly the influence of Napoleon and the French, with a brief introduction on the indigenous intellectual backgrounds of the Risorgimento in the eighteenth century.

320. BERKELEY, G. F. H., *Italy in the Making, 1815–1846* (Cambridge, 1932), Cambridge University Press, 292 pp.
The early story of the Risorgimento revolving chiefly around the revolutionary movement of Mazzini, the reaction of Metternich, the work of Charles Albert of Sardinia, the moderates, Gioberti, D'Azeglio and Balbo, and the papacy of Pius IX. Not enough attention is given to the general literary currents, which were important at the time.

320a. GREENFIELD, KENT ROBERTS, *Economics and Liberalism in the Risorgimento. A Study of Nationalism in Lombardy, 1814–1848* (Baltimore, 1934), John Hopkins Press, xiv, 365 pp.
The author sees a great discrepancy between the attention paid by historians of the Risorgimento to Mazzini and to the actually negligible influence of Mazzini upon the eventual unification of Italy. He has looked for the sources of Cavour's liberal nationalism in the economic and industrial

conditions of the time and in the activities of the liberal journalists and publicists.

321. MARRIOTT, J. A. R., *The Makers of Modern Italy. Napoleon-Mussolini* (Oxford, 1931), Clarendon Press, xii, 228 pp.

A story of Italian unity from the French Revolution to Mussolini. The author fails to take into account all the work of the new Italian scholarship on the Risorgimento, which gives an autochthonous interpretation of the Risorgimento and which finds its beginnings in the period between 1748 and 1789. Marriott still persists in the old tradition of beginning with the French Revolution. He is favorably disposed to Fascism and considers the Lateran Treaty of 1929 as the crowning point of Italian unity.

See also Cantalupo, Roberto, "Enrico Corradini and Italian Nationalism," in the *National Review*, LXXXIII (1924), 767–78; and Vallis, M., "Un Imperialiste italien: Enrico Corradini," in the *Grande Revue*, CIX (1922), 596–622; Nothomb, P., "Enrico Corradini, théoricien du nationalisme italien," in the *Revue Générale*, LIX (1926), 539–60.

322. SOLMI, ARRIGO, *The Making of Modern Italy*, translated with introduction, by Arundel del Re (London, 1925), E. Benn, xxi, 231 pp.

A popular survey definitely influenced by the World War. This is a translation of *Il Risorgimento Italiano, 1814–1918* (Milan, 1919).

323. HAZARD, PAUL, *La Révolution française et les lettres italiennes, 1789–1815* (Paris, 1910), Hachette, xviii, 572 pp.

A classic study of the influence of the French Revolution on Italian intellectual life and on the stimulation of Italian nationalism. Special attention is given to such figures as Monti, Alfieri, Foscolo and Cuoco.

324. BULLE, OSKAR, *Die italienische Einheitsidee in ihrer literarischen Entwicklung, von Parini bis Manzoni* (Berlin, 1893), Paul Hüttig, xii, 345 pp.

The national ideas of Giuseppe Parini, Vittorio Alfieri, Vincenzo Monti, Ugo Foscolo, and Allesandro Manzoni.

See also Bouvy, E., "De Dante à Alfieri. L'Idée de patrie dans la poèsie italienne du xiv au xvii siecle," in the Annales de la Faculté des Lettres de Bordeaux et des Universités du Midi, *Bulletin Italien*, XIV (1914), 285–99; and "Alfieri, Monti, Foscolo. La Poésie patriotique en Italie de 1789 à 1815," *ibid.*, XVII (1917), 36–49; and XVIII (1918), 81–94.

325. GARDNER, EDMUND GARRATT, *The National Idea in Italian Literature* (Manchester, 1921), Manchester University Press, 51 pp.

The author has no real conception of what nationalism is. He merely picks at random some expressions of patriotism in Dante, Petrarch, Machiavelli, Alfieri, Mazzini, Gioberti and Carducci.

326. MEGARO, GAUDENCE, *Vittorio Alfieri. A Forerunner of Italian Nationalism* (New York, 1931), Columbia University Press, 175 pp. "Studies in History, Economics and Public Law," No. 336.

Alfieri is the most typical early exponent of nationalism based on hate. In his case it was hatred of the French. This book is a very able analysis of the nationalistic elements in Alfieri's writings, particularly in the tragedies and *Il Misogallo*, showing the influence of the ancients on his ideas concerning tyranny and liberty, and revealing his passionate demand not only for cultural but for political nationalism in Italy. He is pictured as one of the most important inspirers of the nineteenth-century Risorgimento, influencing alike Catholics and liberals, centralists and federalists.

327. ZBINDEN, JEAN, *Die politischen Ideen des Vincenzo Gioberti. Studie zur Geschichte des Frührisorgiments* (Bern, 1920), Paul Haupt, 96 pp.

A narrative and rather enthusiastic account of the religious nationalist doctrines of Gioberti, as revealed in his writings and public activities.

328. KING, BOLTON, *The Life of Mazzini*, 2d ed. (London, 1911), J. M. Dent, xv, 380 pp. "Everyman's Library".

Despite its age, it is still the best English life of Mazzini, especially from the point of view of a deeper analysis of his ideas and career. Ch. XVII deals specifically with his theories of nationality.

See also Brown, Sydney M., "Mazzini and Dante," in the *Political Science Quarterly*, XLII (1927), 77–98.

329. VOSSLER, OTTO, *Mazzinis politisches Denken und Wollen in den geistigen Strömmungen seiner Zeit*, (Munich, 1927), R. Oldenbourg, 94 pp. *Historische Zeitschrift*, Beiheft XI.

This volume contains a short survey of the national idea in Italy before Mazzini, in which the author attacks the thesis of Napoleon's great influence in inspiring Italian nationalism. It is particularly valuable for tracing the German influence, especially that of Herder, on the early Risorgimento.

Cf. No. 158.

330. VIDAL, C., *Charles-Albert et le Risorgimento italien (1831–1848)* (Paris, 1927), E. de Brocard, 632 pp.

A narrative account of the national policy of Charles Albert of Sardinia and his reactions to the nationalist currents.

331. HANCOCK, W. K., *Ricasoli and the Risorgimento in Tuscany* (London, 1926), Faber and Gwyer, x, 320 pp.

A narrative biography of the leader of the Risorgimento in Tuscany.

325. TREVELYAN, GEORGE MACAULAY, *Garibaldi and the Making of Italy* (London, 1911), Longmans, Green and Co., xx, 390 pp.

A narrative account of the exploits of Garibaldi. There is little in this account to contribute to the understanding of nationalism as such.

333. THAYER' WILLLIAM ROSCOE, *The Life and Times of Cavour*, 2 vols. (Boston, 1911), Houghton Mifflin Co., xvi, 604 pp. and 562 pp.

The classic life of Cavour.

334. MATTER, PAUL, *Cavour et l'unité italienne*, 3 vols. (Paris, 1922–27), Félix Alcan, iv, 364 pp., 415 pp., and 499 pp.

Chiefly an account of the diplomatic and political policies of Cavour.

335. WHYTE, ARTHUR JAMES, *The Political Life and Letters of Cavour, 1848–1861* (London, 1930), Oxford University Press, xv, 478 pp.

This work is chiefly concerned with Cavour's diplomatic career. The author's thesis is that Italian unity was brought about by England, Cavour and Napoleon. The book has been criticized for misinterpretation of Italian texts and for failure to use all available archive material. Cf. the articles by Alessandro Luzio in *Corriera della Serra*, October 11 and 21, 1930.

336. MARRARO, HOWARD R., *American Opinion on the Unification of Italy, 1846–1861* (New York, 1932), Columbia University Press, xii, 345 pp.

An interesting collection of comments and expressions of opinion by Americans on the various stages of the Italian nationalist movement from 1846 to 1861, and the reception accorded to Italian political exiles in America.

On Italian Fascism the following works are the most relevant and most important:

337. SCHNEIDER, HERBERT W., *Making the Fascist State* (New York, 1928), Oxford University Press, 390 pp.

The most comprehensive attempt at studying both the ideology and the

practical political administration of Italian Fascism. It is uneven, however, in its result.
See also Rocco, Alfredo, "The Political Doctrine of Fascism," in *International Conciliation*, No. CCXXIII (1926), which is an official Fascist exposition.

338. STURZO, LUIGI, *Italy and Fascismo*, translated from the Italian by B. B. Carter (London, 1926), Faber and Gwyer, ix, 305 pp.
A profound philosophical interpretation by the leader of the Catholic *Partito Popolare*.

339. HELLER, HERMANN, *Europa und der Fascismus*, 2d ed. (Berlin, 1931), Walter de Gruyter, 159 pp.
This work is by a Socialist critic of Fascism. The author, who reveals a complete mastery of the subject, denies to Fascism any personification of great social or political ideas. The only ideas present, according to him, are opposition to democracy and the will to power over the masses.

340. BECKERATH, ERWIN VON, *Wesen und Werden des fascistischen Staates* (Berlin, 1927), Julius Springer, 155 pp.
This is a solid work, particularly strong on the theoretical and ideological side and without any outspoken tendency. The author treats Fascism, however, with serious respect.

341. BERNHARD, LUDWIG, *Der Staatsgedanke des Fascismus* (Berlin, 1931), Julius Springer, 44 pp.
A very penetrating and objective analysis of Fascist political ideology.

342. SCHNEIDER, HERBERT W., and SHEPARD B. CLOUGH, *Making Fascists* (Chicago, 1929), University of Chicago Press, xv, 211 pp.
One of the volumes in the series, "Studies in the Making of Citizens," edited by Charles Merriam. A study of the infusion into, and utilization of, economic groups, religious institutions, education, the press and patriotic organizations, to develop and foster the nationalistic ideals of Fascism, which are inspired by the ideals of ancient Rome. Regionalism and national symbolism are also discussed.

343. SILONE, IGNAZIO, *Der Fascismus. Seine Entstehung und Entwicklung* (Zürich, 1934), Europa Verlag, 294 pp.
The best social interpretation of Fascism, with very keen general remarks and comparisons on Fascism as a worldwide manifestation. The author is a Left-Socialist.

344. MARRARO, HOWARD R., *Nationalism in Italian Education* (New York, 1927), Italian Digest and News Service, xxviii, 161 pp.
A pro-Fascist account of the nationalist educational reforms of Gentile.

NATIONALISM IN SPAIN, PORTUGAL AND LATIN AMERICA

See also No. 66

For the historical development of Spanish nationalism, the writings of the following are important: Joaquin Costa y Martinés, Angel Ganivet, Lafuente y Zamalloa, Riccardo Macias Picavea, Pi y Margall, and the Catalans Valentin Almirall, Torras y Bages and Enrique Prat de la Riba. For Portugal, the works of Theophil Braga, Jose da Silva Carvalho and Guerro Junqueiro are important.

345. MADARIAGA, SALVADOR DE, *Spain* (London, 1930), Ernest Benn, 507 pp.
Chapters XVI–XVIII, pp. 246–310, contain an admirable discussion of the psychological and historical background of the Catalan question, and an analysis of its present-day significance.

346. DWELSHAUVERS, GEORGES, *La Catalogne et le problème Catalan* (Paris, 1926), Félix Alcan, viii, 236 pp.
A general survey of Catalonia, its language and institutions, and the autonomist movement and the development of a Catalan culture. The author concludes that Catalonia represents an ethnic, economic, cultural and political unity—in short a Catalan nationality.
Important articles on Spain and Latin America are: Jeschke, H., "Angel Ganivet," in the *Revue hispanique,* LXXII (1928), 102–246; Haas, Albert, "Der pan-hispanische Gedanke in Amerika," in the *Zeitschrift für Politik* XVI (1927), 1–31.

NATIONALISM IN GREAT BRITAIN AND THE DOMINIONS

See also Nos. 8, 25, 66, 82, 99, 111, 112, 113.

For the historical development of English nationalism, the writings of the following are important: Henry St. John Bolingbroke, Edmund Burke, Thomas Carlyle, Joseph Chamberlain, Charles W. Dilke, Benjamin Disraeli, Edward A. Freeman, James A. Froude, John R. Green, John M. Kemble, Charles Kingsley, Thomas Babington Macaulay, John Stuart Mill, John Milton, John Ruskin, John R. Seeley and Sharon Turner.

347. OAKESMITH, JOHN, *Race and Nationality. An Inquiry into the Origin and Growth of Patriotism* (London, 1919), Heinemann, xix, 299 pp.
A critique of the theories of an immutable national soul, based on race. Chapters VI–XIV analyze in detail the historical development of English nationality and national literature, showing the variety of cultural traditions that entered into its composition.
See also Hertz, F., "Der englische Nationalismus vor dem Kriege," in *Der Kampf,* XXI (1928), 615–19; Aronstein, Philipp, "Patriotismus und Staatsgefühl der Engländer," in the *Neue Jahrbücher für Wissenschaft und Jugendbildung,* V (1929), 558–78.

348. WINGFIELD-STRATFORD, ESMÉ, *The History of English Patriotism,* 2 vols. (London, 1913), John Lane, xl, 614 pp. and xii, 672 pp.
This work contains a great deal of material on the growth of English national patriotism, but the author has no real understanding of the nature of nationalism and no central concept except a vague religious and mystical antagonism to materialistic philosophies, and a spiritual idealization of patriotism.

349. DRINKWATER, JOHN, *Patriotism in Literature* (London, 1924), Williams and Norgate, ix, 255 pp.
This is a popular study of patriotism, as reflected in the works of poets and novelists. The examples are drawn chiefly from English literature. The author's viewpoint is a positive affirmation of patriotism as "a spiritual force, a mood, an energy that aims at no material advantages, a delight as natural and as uncalculating as the pleasure we take in sunlight or sound limbs."

350. BOUTMY, ÉMILE, *The English People. A Study of Their Political Psychology,* translated from the French by E. English, with introduction by J. E. C. Bodley (New York, 1904), G. P. Putnam's Sons, xxxvi, 332 pp.
One of the more serious attempts, by a disciple of Taine, to present a general view of English national psychology and English political traits.

351. GAUS, JOHN MERRIMAN, *Great Britain. A Study of Civic Loyalty* (Chicago, 1929), University of Chicago Press, xxi, 329 pp.
A volume in the series, "Studies in the Making of Citizens," edited by Charles Merriam. For nationalism in Great Britain, the chapters on

the king, the empire, the school system, the press and the church as forces molding nationalist opinion are relevant.

352. EINSTEIN, LEWIS, *Tudor Ideals* (New York, 1921), Harcourt, Brace and Company, xiii, 366 pp.
Part III, Ch. III, and Part IV, Chs. IX, X, XI and XIII, present a discussion of the beginnings of English patriotism and national feeling, and their interaction with a new cosmopolitanism. This interaction, the author holds, was responsible for the flowering of English civilization in the Elizabethan period.

353. COBBAN, ALFRED, *Edmund Burke and the Revolt against the Eighteenth Century* (London, 1929), Allen and Unwin, 280 pp.
Chapter IV is a discussion of Burke's nationalist views. The major part of the book is a discussion of the reaction in England against sensationalism in psychology, naturalism in religion, utilitarianism in ethics, individualism in economics, and cosmopolitanism in politics. Wordsworth, Coleridge and Southey are also discussed in these connections.
See also Hayes, Carlton J. H., "Bolingbroke: the Philosopher Turned Patriot," in *Essays in Intellectual History* (New York, 1929), pp. 189–206.

354. FAIRCHILD, HOXIE NEALE, *The Romantic Quest* (New York, 1931), Columbia University Press, viii, 444 pp.
While almost exclusively a literary study, this work is valuable for the intellectual backgrounds of British Romanticism and nationalism. Of particular importance are Ch. VI on Romantic intellectualism and Chs. XIV, XV and XVI on the medievalism of Scott, and on Wordsworth, Coleridge and Keats.

355. PEARDON, THOMAS PRESTON, *The Transition in English Historical Writing, 1760–1830* (New York, 1933), Columbia University Press, 340 pp. "Studies in History, Economics and Public Law," No. 390.
This study shows the turn from rationalist cosmopolitan history to nationalist history, and traces the influence of primitivism and medievalism.

356. KAYSER, ELMER LOUIS, *The Grand Social Enterprise, a Study of Jeremy Bentham in His Relation to Liberal Nationalism* (New York, 1932), Columbia University Press, 109 pp. "Studies in History, Economics and Public Law," No. 377.
The works of Bentham, the supreme exponent of liberal nationalism, were seized upon by a considerable number of active nationalists in the early nineteenth century and became their textbooks and models for legislation. In this way the utilitarian liberalism of Bentham was joined with the Romantic nationalism, and thus constituted an important factor in the liberal nationalism which was so conspicuous among the "oppressed" peoples in the middle of the nineteenth century. This was not a chauvinistic nationalism. It recognized the validity of nationalities and claimed for each the right of self-determination. But liberal principles were to govern the nation and its relations with other nations.

357. BODELSEN, C. A., *Studies in Mid-Victorian Imperialism* (Copenhagen, 1924), Nordisk forlag, 230 pp.
There are some revealing pages on the heroic nationalism of Carlyle, on the racial Anglo-Saxonism of Charles Wentworth Dilke, on the expansionism and idealization of the national state by Seely, and on the "social" imperialism of Froude. The author points out the complete neglect by all these writers of colonial nationalism.

358. BATTEN, EDWARD, *Nationalism, Politics and Economics* (London, 1929), P. S. King, 145 pp.
Mainly a discussion of the influence of economic nationalism on British

economic policy, and suggesting means of adjusting British policy to the growing economic nationalism of other countries.

359. HACKETT, FRANCIS, *Ireland. A Study in Nationalism*, 4th ed. (New York, 1920), B. W. Huebsch, xx, 395 pp.
Despite its immediate relation to the events of the time, this volume is still valuable for an analysis of the various factors in Irish nationalism, especially the economic factor. While an Irish nationalist, the author is also fully alive to the danger of nationalist policy.

360. CLARKSON, J. DUNSMORE, *Labour and Nationalism in Ireland* (New York, 1925), Columbia University Press, 502 pp. "Studies in History, Economics and Public Law," No. 266.
A very good interpretation of Irish nationalism from the viewpoint of the labor movement and an attempt to correlate the development of the labor movement with the nationalist struggle. The author takes up the attitudes toward labor within the leading nationalist currents and the share of labor in the nationalist movement. He is concerned more with urban than with rural labor. His thesis is that the national aspirations of Ireland "derived their motive power from oppression."

361. HANLY, JOSEPH, *The National Ideal. A Practical Exposition of True Nationality Appertaining to Ireland* (London, 1932), Sands, xvi, 275 pp.
A propagandistic work by an extreme Irish nationalist, for the complete "Gaelicization" of Irish life in all its political, economic and cultural aspects.

362. SHEEHY-SKEFFINGTON, F., *Michael Davitt, Revolutionary, Agitator and Labour Leader* (London, 1908), T. Fisher Unwin, xix, 291 pp.
The best life of the most important leader of Irish laborite and agrarian nationalism. It is strongly anti-Catholic in sentiment.
Cf. J. Keir Hardie and T. M. Kettle on Davitt in the *Socialist Review*, I (1908) 410–21.

363. BEASLEY, PIERCE, (Béaslái, Piaras), *Michael Collins and the Making of a New Ireland*, 2 vols. (London, 1926), George Harrap and Co., xv, 458 pp. and 484 pp.
An enthusiastic and intensely nationalistic biography, by an intimate friend of Collins. It is primarily a factual account of the later stages of the Sinn Fein movement.

364. GWYNN, DENIS R., *Edward Martyn and the Irish Revival* (London, 1928), Champion, iv, 384 pp.
The story of one of the leading figures in the national Irish literary and artistic movement.

365. WALLACE, WILLIAM STEWART, *The Growth of Canadian National Feeling* (Toronto, 1927), Macmillan, 85 pp.
The author affirms the existence of an All-Canadian nationalism which, though young, is the product of historical conditions and political unity. See also Ziehen, Edward, "Canadianism. Zur Genesis der kanadischen Nation," in the *Historische Zeitschrift*, CL (1934), 497–558.

366. VATTIER, GEORGES, *Essai sur la mentalité canadienne-française* (Paris, 1928), Champion, iv, 384 pp.
A study of French-Canadian national psychology by a Frenchman who looks upon the French-Canadians as French by nationality. Pages 245–378 are particularly important for their treatment of the attitude of French-Canadians toward France, England, the United States, and the problem of autonomy.
Cf. No. 57.

NATIONALISM IN THE UNITED STATES
See also Nos. 8, 84, 99, 111, 384

For nationalism in the United States, the writings of the following are important: George Bancroft, Edward Bellamy, Charles Beard, Randolph Bourne, Henry Clay, Herbert Croly, Madison Grant John Hay, Homer Lea, Francis Lieber, Walter Hines Page, Francis Parkman, W. H. Prescott, Theodore Roosevelt, Lothrop Stoddard and Woodrow Wilson.

367. BOUTMY, ÉMILE, *Éléments d'une psychologie politique du peuple américain* (Paris, 1920), Armand Colin, xl, 367 pp.
A semijournalistic but very interesting discussion of the American feeling of nationality (see particularly pp. 77–105).
See also Michels, Roberto, "Über den amerikanischen Nationalitätsbegriff," in the *Weltwirtschaftliches Archiv*, XXVIII (1928) 257–99."

368. HUMPHREY, EDWARD FRANK, *Nationalism and Religion in America, 1774–89* (Boston, 1924), Chipman Law Publishing Co., viii, 536 pp.
The author's object is to throw light on the part religion played in creating an American nationalism.

369. FAIRCHILD, HENRY PRATT, *The Melting-Pot Mistake* (Boston, 1926), Little, Brown and Co., vi, 266 pp.
A denial of the possibility of the assimilation of alien racial and national elements into American life, and a plea for the maintenance of American group unity by a strong check on alien immigration and alien influences.

370. DRACHSLER, JULIUS, *Democracy and Assimilation* (New York, 1920), Macmillan, xii, 275 pp.
An American Jewish sociologist analyzes the problem of the clash of nationalities among immigrant groups in the United States, their intermarriage and the attempts at assimilation. He urges the broadening of the concept of democracy to include also cultural autonomy and democracy for alien cultural groups.

371. KALLEN, HORACE MEYER, *Culture and Democracy in the United States. Studies in the Group Psychology of the American Peoples* (New York, 1924), Boni and Liveright, 347 pp.
The case for cultural pluralism in the United States.

372. GALITZI, C., *A Study of Assimilation among the Roumanians in the United States* (New York, 1929), Columbia University Press, 284 pp.
A study of the interaction of two national cultures, and the effect on Rumanian national characteristics and peculiarities of their contacts and transplantation to American soil. The author raises the problem of national and ethnic assimilation and Americanization. The book is a good source of information on Rumanian national customs and characteristics.

373. HAPGOOD, N., editor, *Professional Patriots* (New York, 1927), Albert and Charles Boni, vii, 217 pp.
An exposé of the nationalistic and patriotic propaganda carried on by organizations in the United States, such as the National Civic Federation, National Security League, American Defense Society, American Legion, their connections with business, military organizations and labor, and their influence on education.

374. PIERCE, BESSIE LOUISE, *Civic Attitudes in American School Textbooks* (Chicago, 1930), University of Chicago Press, vxi, 297 pp.

A volume in the series, "Studies in the Making of Citizens," edited by Charles Merriam. A study of textbooks in history, civics, sociology, economic and political problems, geography, reading, music and foreign languages, used in elementary and high schools in various states of the Union, showing the attitudes toward other nationalities and the ideals of Americanism indoctrinated into the minds of the young.

375. PIERCE, BESSIE LOUISE, *Citizens' Organizations and the Civic Training of Youth*, Part III of the *Report of the Commission on the Social Studies of the American Historical Association* (New York, 1933), Charles Scribner's Sons, xvii, 428 pp.
A very valuable report of the influence on the teaching of history and civics in the schools of the United States by various patriotic organizations, military groups, peace organizations, fraternal orders, religious and racial groups, youth movements, business and labor groups and prohibition and antiprohibition groups.

376. TURNER, FREDERICK J., *The Significance of Sections in American History* (New York, 1933), Henry Holt, ix, 347 pp.
A regionalist approach to American history.
Cf. the review by L. M. Hacker in the *Nation*, CXXXVII (1933), 108–10.

377. BEARD, CHARLES A., *The Idea of National Interest. An Analytical Study in American Foreign Policy* (New York, 1934), Macmillan, ix, 583 pp.
An inquiry into "the things and patterns of conduct covered by the formula national interest" in their American development from 1787 to the present, as revealed in the Constitution of the United States, and in territorial and commercial expansion.
See also Shepardson, Whitney H., "Nationalism and American Trade," in *Foreign Affairs*, XII (1934), 403–17.

377a. BEARD, CHARLES A., *The Open Door at Home; A Trial Philosophy of National Interest* (New York, 1934), Macmillan, 331 pp.
This is the most significant attempt at a formulation of a philosophy of liberal nationalism as a basis for American public policy.

NATIONALISM IN THE ORIENT

GENERAL STUDIES ON THE ORIENT

See also Nos. 8, 19

378. KOHN, HANS, *A History of Nationalism in the East*, translated from the German by Margaret M. Green, (London, 1929), Routledge, xi, 476 pp.
The most authoritative study of the national movements in Egypt, Turkey, Arabia, Persia, Afghanistan and India, and their relations to Great Britain and Russia. The book is most valuable for the study of nationalist ideology. The author is chiefly concerned with the development of the national *idea*, and traces movements in the East analogous to those in Europe between the seventeenth and nineteenth centuries.

379. KOHN, HANS, *Die Europäisierung des Orients* (Berlin, 1934), Schocken Verlag, 356 pp.
The author presents a most interesting analysis of the process of the Europeanization of the Orient. He considers this process in large measure the equivalent to the emergence of Western Europe from medievalism, and he shows clearly how this progress of Europeaniza-

tion, industrialization and secularization has contributed to the development of nationalism in the Orient.

380. GROUSSET, RENÉ, *Le Reveil de l'Asie; l'impérialisme brittanique et la révolte des peuples* (Paris, 1924), Plon, 251 pp.
This volume takes up Turkish, Egyptian, Hindu and Persian nationalism and the relations thereof to Great Britain. The author attributes the check to British domination to British failure to understand the legitimate needs of the native peoples.

381. EDDY, GEORGE SHERWOOD, *The Challenge of the East* (New York, 1931), Farrar and Rinehart, xx, 265 pp.
An account of the political unrest and national movements in India, China, Japan, Korea, the Philippines, Turkey and Palestine, by a pacifist Socialist journalist with a deep sympathy for the native national movements and a decided anti-imperialist attitude.

NATIONALISM IN THE NEAR EAST

For the historical development of nationalism in the Near East, the writings of the following are important: for Egypt, Jamal al-Din al-Afghani, Muhamad Abduh, Muhammad Rashid Rida, Mustapha Kemal and Abdullah al-Mamun Suhrawardy; for Turkey, Jussuf Bey Akstchura Gasprinskis, Schinasi Effendi and Zia Gök Alp; for Syria and Arabia, Butros el Bustani.

382. KOHN, HANS, *Nationalism and Imperialism in the Hither East*, translated from the German by Margaret M. Green (London, 1932), Routledge, viii, 339 pp.
A detailed study of the nationalist movements in Egypt, Palestine, Transjordania, Syria and Iraq.

383. YOUNG, GEORGE, *Nationalism and War in the Near East* (Oxford, 1915), Clarendon Press, xxvi, 428 pp.
This book, written before the World War, was published anonymously by the Carnegie Endowment for International Peace under the pseudonym "Diplomatist." The author's view is that nationalism is the "main motive of the history of Western Europe of yesterday and of Eastern Europe to-day." He analyzes in this light the eastern question, the Macedonian problem, the Turkish national movement, and the wars resulting from these conflicts. Although much of the book is now outdated, the historical sections are still valuable.

384. PAGE, KIRBY, *Imperialism and Nationalism. A Study of Conflict in the Near East and of the Territorial and Economic Expansion of the United States* (New York, 1925), George H. Doran, vii, 92 pp.
Chapters I–III present a very sketchy and unoriginal account of the conflicts of nationality in the Balkans and Turkey. The rest of the book is an attack on aggressive American national expansion, and a plea for international coöperation.

385. CHIROL, VALENTINE, *The Egyptian Problem* (London, 1920), Macmillan, xii, 331 pp.
This work is chiefly political, but it also has a short résumé of the genesis of Egyptian nationalism from the time of Mehemet Ali. It stresses the benefits of British rule, but tries also to be fair to the Egyptian nationalists.

386. GAULIS, B. G., *Le Nationalisme égyptien* (Paris, 1928), Berger-Levrault, 205 pp.
A collection of periodical articles concerned with the events of the years 1924–27.

387. SABRY, MOUSTAPHA, *La Genèse de l'esprit national égyptien, 1853–1882* (Paris, 1924), Rene Picart, 288 pp.
Important chiefly for the treatment of the contacts of Egypt with Europe, its Europeanization, and the effects on the rise of a nationalist movement.

388. ADAMS, CHARLES C., *Islam and Modernism in Egypt. A Study of the Modern Reform Movement Inaugurated by Muhammad Abduh* (London, 1933), Oxford University Press, ix, 283 pp.
While primarily devoted to the analysis of changes in Moslem theological doctrines, this book is valuable as revealing the connections between modernism and westernization and the growth of nationalism and Pan-Islamism in the Near East. It deals chiefly with the life and works of Muhammad Abduh and Muhammad Rashid Rida, but also has a good chapter on their spiritual father, Jamal Al-Din Al-Afghani and another on the younger Egyptian modernists.
Cf. also Horten, M., "Muhammed Abduh," in *Beiträge zur Kenntnis des Orients*, XIII (1916), 83–114, and XIV (1917), 74–128.

389. BROCKELMANN, KARL, *Das Nationalgefühl der Türken im Licht der Geschichte* (Halle, 1918), Max Niemeyer, 22 pp. "Hallische Universitätsreden," No. X.
A very brief survey of the major currents in Turkish nationalism from early times to the present.
See also No. 53, and Deny, J., "Zia Goek Alp," in the *Revue du monde mussulman*, LXI (1925), 1–41.

390. EMIN, A., *Development of Modern Turkey as Measured by Means of the Press* (New York, 1914), Columbia University Press, 143 pp. "Studies in History, Economics and Public Law," No. 142.
This is a detailed study of the development of the press in Turkey, and its influence on the growth of the nationalist movement.

391. GAULIS, B. G., *La Question arabe* (Paris, 1930), Berger-Levrault, 309 pp.
A journalistic account of the activities of Ibn Saud, the Wahabi movement, Syrian nationalism and its relation to the French mandate.

392. MACCALLUM, ELIZABETH, *The Nationalist Crusade in Syria* (New York, 1928), The Foreign Policy Association, xii, 299 pp.
Almost exclusively concerned with political events in Syria and their relations to France as the mandatory of Syria.
For nationalism in Armenia and Georgia, see Boyajian, Zabelle C., "Raffi: The Armenian National Writer," in the *Contemporary Review*, CX (1916), 223–28; and Van Gennep, Arnold, "La Nationalité géorgienne: les causes de sa formation et de son maintien," in the *Revue de l'Institut de Sociologie*, I, No. 3 (1920), 7–46.

NATIONALISM IN THE FAR EAST

See also Nos. 19, 99, 112

For the historical development of nationalism in China, the writings of the following are important: K'ang Yu We, Li'ang Ch'i Ch'ao, Sun Yat Sen and Hu Shih; for Japan, Kada, Mabuchi, Motoori and Okuma.

393. VINACKE, HAROLD M., *A History of the Far East in Modern Times;* 2d ed. (New York, 1933), F. S. Crofts, xv, 502 pp.
This is chiefly a political history of the Far East, but Chs. XIII, XV, XVI, XVIII and XXII contain good summary treatments of the development of Chinese and Japanese nationalism, both in the political and cultural spheres.

See also Suranyi-Ungar, T., "Wirtschaft und Nationalismus im fernen Osten," in the *Zeitschrift für die gesammte Staatwissenschaft*, LXXXIX (1920), 278–311; and Sato, E. M., "The Revival of Pure Shinto," in Asiatic Society, *Transactions* III (1874), Appendix.

394. OWEN, DAVID EDWARD, *Imperialism and Nationalism in the Far East* (New York, 1929), Henry Holt, xii, 128 pp.
A brief summary of the westernization and growth of nationalism in China and Japan, with considerable attention to intellectual and cultural currents.

395. HOLCOMBE, ARTHUR N., *The Chinese Revolution. A Phase in the Regeneration of a World Power* (Cambridge, 1930), Harvard University Press, xiii, 401 pp.
The most competent study of recent developments in China, providing an extensive interpretation of Sun Yat Sen's theories and the work of the Kuomingtang.

396. T'ANG LEANG-LI, *China in Revolt. How a Civilization Became a Nation* (London, 1927), Noel Douglas, xvii, 176 pp.
The best work by a Chinese scholar on the Chinese national problem, treated mainly from the aspect of relations with the western powers.

397. T'ANG LEANG-LI, *The Foundations of Modern China* (London, 1928) Noel Douglas, x, 290 pp.
An excellent complement to the author's *China in Revolt*, treating of the internal development of the Chinese national movement, the intellectual revolution, the work of Sun Yat Sen and the Kuomingtang, and the influence of western culture.

398. PEAKE, CYRUS H., *Nationalism and Education in Modern China* (New York, 1932), Columbia University Press, xiv, 240 pp.
A survey of the far-reaching revolution in education since 1860. The second part deals with the indoctrination of nationalism in the Chinese government schools by the use of nationalist textbooks.

399. ROY, MANABENDRA NATH, *Revolution und Konterrevolution in China*, translated from the English manuscript by Paul Fröhlich (Berlin, 1930), Soziologische Verlagsanstalt, 480 pp.
A Marxist interpretation of the Chinese nationalist movement. The author was for a long time active in China on behalf of the Communist International and much of his work is based on personal observations and experiences. Of particular interest is his class interpretation of the nationalist ideology of Sun Yat Sen and the Kuomingtang.

400. RODES, JEAN, *La Chine nationaliste, 1912–1930* (Paris, 1931), Félix Alcan, v, 193 pp.
Chiefly a narration of political 'events.

NATIONALISM IN INDIA

See also Nos. 8, 19

For the historical development of nationalism in India, the writings of the following are important: Mahatma Gandhi, G. K. Gokhale, Dadabhoy Naoroji, Lajpat Rai, Ram Mohan Ray, Mahadeo G. Ranade, S. D. Saraswati, Bal G. Tilak, and Swami Vivekenanda.

401. POLE, D. GRAHAM, *India in Transition* (London, 1932), Leonard and Virginia Woolf, xii, 395 pp.
A lucid presentation of the facts of the Indian national struggle and the British-Indian relations by one in sympathy with the Indian national

aspirations. The volume covers political events, economic conditions, administrative measures, etc.

402. TOPA, ISHWAR NATH, *The Growth and Development of National Thought in India* (Hamburg, 1930), J. J. Augustin, xiv, 176 pp.
The economic and political background of the Indian nationalist movement and the story of the movement up to 1918.

403. CHITAMBAR, JASHWANT R., *Mahatma Gandhi, His Life, Work and Influence* (Philadelphia, 1933), John C. Winston, xvii, 266 pp.
An uncritical account of the life and activities of India's most famous nationalist.

404. BANNERJEA, D. N., *India's Nation Builders* (London, 1919), Headly Bros., 234 pp.
Short sketches of Tagore, Ram Mohan Roy, Keshab Chandra Sen, Dayananda Saraswati, Syèd Ahmad Kahn, Dadabhoy Naoroji, Vivekananda, Gokhale, Gandhi, Banuyi, Tilak, Chandra Pal, Ghose, Lala Lajpat Rai, and Surendranath Bannerjea.

405. ROY, MANABENDRA NATH, *Indien*, translated from the English manuscript by W. S. Schulz (Hamburg, 1922), C. Hoym, xv, 191 pp.
A Communist exposition of the national movement in India in which the nationalist ideology is interpreted as only an intellectual superstructure for the economic and social interests of the democratic bourgeoisie.

406. DUTT, R. PALME, *Modern India* (London, 1927), Communist Party of Great Britain, 174 pp.
A Communistic interpretation of the Indian national movement as an anticapitalist, and anti-imperialist movement for better living conditions. The specifically "national" elements are denied as too vague and undefinable.

407. LAJPAT RAI, *Young India. An Interpretation and a History of the Nationalist Movement from Within*, 2d ed. (New York, 1917), B. W. Huebsch, xxvi, 257 pp.
A history of the nationalist movement in India by one of the leaders of the extreme wing of the Indian nationalist movement, colored by a deeply religious tinge of the *Vedas* and the *Upanishads*.

408. MOOKERJI, RADHAKUMUD, *Nationalism in Hindu Culture* (London, 1921), Theosophical Publishing House, ix, 104 pp.
A very popular series of lectures on patriotism and nationalism in Sanskrit literature.

409. RAY, PRITHWIS CHAKDRA, *Life and Times of C. R. Das* (London, 1927), Oxford University Press, xvi, 313 pp.
A biography of the famous bourgeois liberal Bengal National leader. The work fails, however, to go deeply into the various transformations which Das underwent.

NATIONALISM AMONG THE JEWS
See also Nos. 8, 44, 52

For the historical development of Jewish nationalism, the writings of the following are important: Ber Borochov, Martin Buber, S. M., Dubnow, Achad Haam (Asher Ginzberg), A. D. Gordon, Theodor Herzl, Moses Hess, Moses L. Lillienblum, Max Nordau, Leo Pinsker, and Chayim Zhitlovsky.

410. KOHN, HANS, *Nationalismus. Über die Bedeutung des Nationalismus im Judentum und in der Gegenwart* (Vienna, 1922), R. Löwit Verlag, 128 pp.

A collection of essays on Zionism, Achad Haam, nationalism in Asia, and a general essay on the theory of nationalism.

411. RUPPIN, A., *Soziologie der Juden*, 2 vols. (Berlin, 1930–31), Jüdischer Verlag, 522 pp. and 336 pp.
Chapters I–IV deal with the racial composition of the Jews and their national characteristics; Ch. XXVI with the Jews as a national minority; Chs. XXXI–XXXVIII with the question of Jewish national survival; and Ch. XXXIX with the question of Zionism.

412. KLATZKIN, J., *Probleme des modernen Judentums*, 3d ed. (Berlin, 1930), Lambert Schneider, 208 pp.
A discussion of Jewish assimilation, Diaspora nationalism and Zionism, by a keen philosophic Hebraist and Zionist.

413. JANOWSKY, OSCAR I., *The Jews and Minority Rights, 1898–1919* (New York, 1933), Columbia University Press, 421 pp. "Studies in History, Economics and Public Law," No. 384.
This is the only book of its kind in any language and perhaps the most important book on the subject of Jewish nationalism in the English language. It gives an admirable survey of the intellectual development of Jewish nationalism and the organizations formed to further it. Whereas Zionism has often been treated, the various currents working for national autonomy have never been adequately treated before. The work of Zhitlowsky, Dubnow, the Bund, the Poale Zion and Borochov and all the other factions and currents are discussed in a most intelligent fashion. The effects of the Russian Revolution and activity after the World War are presented in a dramatic style. The author draws on unprinted material and oral communication with many of the leaders involved. The influence of Jewish activity on the minority provisions in the postwar treaties is clearly brought out, as is the significance of the Jews as a nonterritorial nationality.

414. KAUTSKY, KARL, *Are the Jews a Race?* translated from the 2d German ed. (New York, 1926), International Publishers, 256 pp.
This book is directed against racial anti-Semitism on the one hand and against Jewish nationalism and Zionism on the other. The author predicts the disappearance of the Jews as a distinct entity.

415. BLITZ, SAMUEL, *Nationalism, a Cause of Anti-Semitism* (New York, 1928), Bloch Publishing Co., xiii, 157 pp.
A rather superficial survey of anti-Semitism since earliest times, reducing it all to the clash between an international Jewry and the nationalistic aspirations of the dominant groups.

416. KOHN, HANS, *L'Humanisme juif. Quinze essais sur le juif, le monde et Dieu* (Paris, 1931), Rieder, 276 pp.
Contains very illuminating essays on Herzl, Nathan Birnbaum, Moses Hess, Achad Haam, A. D. Gordon and Martin Buber.

417. BÖHM, ADOLF, *Die zionistische Bewegung*, 2 vols. (Berlin, 1920–21), Welt Verlag, 190 pp. and 364 pp.
A very able survey of the Zionist movement from its precursors to the postwar period. It is good both on the ideological and on the practical organizational and socio-economic aspects.

418. HOLDHEIM, GERHARD, and WALTER PREUSS, *Die theoretischen Grundlagen des Zionismus* (Berlin, 1919), Welt Verlag, 82 pp.
A good, brief historical summary of the leading Jewish nationalist doctrines from earliest times to the present, and a systematic study of the relations of Zionism to such other problems as socialism, imperialism, cosmopolitanism, anti-Semitism, assimilation, religious ideas, and ethnic considerations. The authors are Zionists.

419. STEIN, LEONARD, *Zionism* (London, 1925), Ernest Benn, vii, 218 pp.
A concise account of the history, aims and achievements of the Zionist movement by an official Zionist publicist.

420. SIMON, LEON, *Studies in Jewish Nationalism* (London, 1920), Longmans, Green and Co., xi, 174 pp.
A collection of essays on Jewish nationalism and religion, particularly concerned with Hebraism, Zionism and Palestine. The author is a leading Anglo-Zionist publicist.

421. MARGULIES, HEINRICH, *Kritik der Zionismus*, 2 vols. (Vienna, 1920), R. Löwit, Vol. I, *Volk und Gemeinschaft*, 171 pp.; Vol. II, *Der Zionismus als Volksbewegung*, 267 pp.
On the basis of an elaborate sociological and philosophical analysis of national group feeling outlined in the first volume, the author presents, in his second volume, a detailed theoretical critique of Jewish nationalist ideologies, and attempts to set up a synthesis of Palestinian Zionism and Diaspora nationalism.

422. ZLOCISTI, THEODOR, *Moses Hess der Vorkämpfer des Sozialismus und Zionismus*, 2d ed. (Berlin, 1921), Welt Verlag, 441 pp.
The best work on one of the earliest theorists of Jewish nationalism. His views on Judaism are discussed, together with his place and activities in pre-Marxian socialism.

423. HAAS, JACOB DE, *Theodor Herzl*, 2 vols. (Chicago, 1927), The Leonard Co., 371 pp. and 376 pp.
A full life of the founder of political Zionism. The author was Herzl's secretary and is a leading American political Zionist.

424. GINSBERG, ASHER, (Achad Haam), *Ten Essays on Zionism and Judaism*, translated from the Hebrew by Leon Simon (London, 1922), George Routledge and Sons, xxiii, 256 pp.
A translation of some of the most important essays by the leading philosopher of cultural Zionism.

425. BUBER, MARTIN, *Die Jüdische Bewegung. Gesammelte Aufsätze und Ansprachen, 1916–1920*, 2 vols. (Berlin, 1920), Jüdischer Verlag, 254 pp. and 223 pp.
Collected essays on Jewish nationalism by the leading German Jewish theoretician of Zionism. The essays cover a wide range of topics, including theoretical discussions of nationalism, Hebrew literature, Jewish national art and Jewish traditionalism. The polemical articles addressed to Hermann Cohen on the theories of Jewish nationalism (Vol. II, pp. 26–70) are particularly important. In connection with this, see Cohen, Hermann, *Jüdische Schriften*, 3 vols. (Berlin, C. A. Schwetschke und Sohn, 1924), Vol. II, pp. 318–40.

426. KOHN, HANS, *Martin Buber, sein Werk und seine Zeit. Ein Versuch über Religion und Politik* (Hellerau, 1930), Jakob Hegner, 411 pp.
An exhaustive study of the most important philosopher of nationalism in German Jewry.

427. SPIEGEL, SHALOM, *Hebrew Reborn* (New York, 1930), Macmillan, 479 pp.
A very able and sympathetic account of the Hebrew literary and linguistic renaissance and its connections with the growth of the Zionist movement.

428. KLAUSNER, JOSEPH, *A History of Modern Hebrew Literature (1785–1930)*, translated from the Hebrew by Herbert Danby (London, 1932), M. L. Cailingold, v, 204 pp.
This is a textbook of Hebrew literature, but Chs. IV–VI present a discussion of the neo-Hebraic literature in terms of the Jewish national revival.

429. BIRNBAUM, N., *Ausgewählte Schriften zur jüdischen Frage*, 2 vols. (Czernowitz, 1910), Buchhandlung Dr. Birnbaum und Dr. Kohut, 336 pp. and 397 pp.

Collected older writing of one of the most important theorists of Jewish nationalism. These include writings on Jewish autonomy, Zionism and the language question.

430. BOROCHOV, BER, *Sozialismus und Zionismus. Eine Synthese*, edited by Mendel Singer (Vienna, 1932), Verlag Zukunft, 398 pp.

Collected essays by the leading theoretician of the Socialist-Zionist movement, who gives a class interpretation of anti-Semitism and Jewish nationalism, and who seeks to harmonize international Marxism with Jewish nationalism. The volume also contains a series of articles on Borochov by M. A. Borochov, J. Ben-Zwi, S. Kaplansky and S. Her. See also the author's *Klasse und Nation: Zur Theorie und Praxis des jüdischen Sozialismus* (Berlin, 1932), Hechaluz, 108 pp; and the articles by A. Tartakower, "Zur Geschichte des jüdischen Sozialismus," in *Der Jude*, VII (1923), 503–16, 591–618, and VIII (1924), 16–38, 148–73, 386–99, 455–72.

431. DUBNOW, S. M., *Die Grundlagen des Nationaljudentums*, Partial translations from the Russian by I. Friedlaender (Berlin, 1905), Jüdischer Verlag, 69 pp.; and by Elias Hurwicz, "Das Alte und das neue Judentum, in *Der Jude*, Sonderheft No. 3 (Berlin, 1926), pp. 32–57.

The theoretical exposition of Jewish Diaspora nationalism, by its leading exponent.

Cf. Friedlaender, Israel, "Dubnow's Theory of Jewish Nationalism," in his *Past and Present* (Cincinnati, 1919), Ark Publishing Co., pp. 371–98.

INDEX OF NAMES

Achad Haam, See Ginsberg, A.

Acton, Lord, "Nationality," 86

Adams, C. C. *Islam and Modernism in Egypt*, 388

Albrecht, G., "Die Ausgestaltung des Listschen Nationalitätsprinzips . . . ," 199

Alembert, d', 263

Alfieri, V., 323, 324, 325, 326

Allport, F. H., "Psychology of Nationalism," 59

Ammende, E., *Die Nationalitaten in den Staaten Europas*, 116

Andler, C., . . . *Le Pangermanisme*, 151

Anin, M., *Die Nationalitatenprobleme der Gegenwart* . . . , 44

Antonowytsch, M., *Friedrich Ludwig Jahn* . . ., 186

Apponyi, Count, 77

Aristotle, 125

Arndt. E. M., 151, 184

Aronstein, P., "Patriotismus und Staatsgefühl der Engländer," 347

Artois, J., d', "Die nationale Entwicklung der Wallonen," 54

Astros, P.-T.-D. d', 270

Aucamp, A. J., *Bilingual Education and Nationalism* . . . , 82

Auerbach, B., *Les Races et les nationalités en Autriche-Hongrie*, 217

Aulard, A., *Le Patriotisme française* . . . , 263

Azelglio, M., d', 320

Baasch, E., "Die deutschen wirtschaftlichen Einheitsbestrebungen . . . ," 199

Bährens, K., *Flanderns Kampf* . . . , 303

Balbo, Cesare, 320

Bannerjea, D. N., *India's Nation Builders*, 404

Bannerjea, S., 404

Banuyi, 404

Barère, Bertrand, 267

Barker, Ernest, *National Character* . . . , 25; *Christianity and Nationality*, 74

Barnes, H. E., *History and Social Intelligence*, 55; ". . . Gustave Le Bon . . . ," 62

Barrès, M., 130, 273, 275, 278

Barth, P., *Die Philosophie der Geschichte* . . . , 16; "Die Nationalität in ihrer soziologischer Bedeutung," 49

Barzun, J., *The French Race*, 258

Basch, V., *Les Doctrines politiques des philosophes classiques de l'Allemagne* . . . , 160

Batten, E., *Nationalism, Politics and Economics*, 358

Battifol. L., 77

Bauer, Johannes, *Schleiermacher als politischer Prediger* . . . , 181

Bauer, Otto. *Die Nationalitätenfrage und die Sozialdemokratie*, 106; 10, 107

Baxa, J., . . . *Romantische Staatswissenschaft*, 172

Beard, Charles A., *The Idea of National Interest* . . . , 377; *The Open Door at Home*, 377a

Beasley, P., *Michael Collins* . . . , 363

Becker, M. L., "Die französische Volksbühne . . . ," 274

Beckerath, E. von, *Wesen und Werden des fascistischen Staates*, 340

Begtrup, H., *The Folk High Schools of Denmark* . . . , 311

Belloc, H., 77

Benda, J., *The Treason of the Intellectuals*, 21; *La Fin de l'éternel*, 22; *Discours à la nation européene*, 23; *Esquisse d'une histoire des Français* . . . , 259

Benson, A. B., *The Old Norse Element in Swedish Romanticism*, 310

Bentham, J., 130, 356

Berkeley, G. F. H., *Italy in the Making, 1815–1846*, 320

Berl, E., review of Julien Benda, 259

Berlet, C., *Les Tendances unitaires et provincialistes en France* . . . , 288

Bernatzik, E., *Die Augestaltung des Nationalgefühls* . . . , 223

Berndt. F., "Nationalitätenfragen in Finnland," 52

Berney, A., "Reichstradition und Nationalstraatsgedanke . . . ," 153

Bernhard, L., *Der Staatsgedanke des Fascismus*, 341

Bernhardi, F. von, 151, 207a

Bernstein, Eduard, 49

Biehahn, W., "Marxismus und nationale Idee . . . ," 244

Biester, J. E., 157

Binder, J., "Fichte und die Nation," 164

Birnbaum, N., 416; *Ausgewählte Schriften* . . . , 429

Bismarck, 139, 145, 151, 200. 207a

Blagoyévitch, V., *Le Principe des nationalités* . . . , 47

Bley, F., 151

Blitz, S., *Nationalism, a Cause of Anti-Semitism*, 415

Blondel, M., 77

Bluntschli, J. K., *The Theory of the State*, 85; *Kleine Schriften*, 48; 152

Boas, F., *Anthropology and Modern Life*, 31

Bodelsen, C. A., *Mid-Victorian Imperialism*, 357

Boehm, M. H., *Das eigenständige Volk* . . . , 7; "Die Nationalitätenfrage," 50; *Ethnopolitischer Almanach*, 52; "Staatsgewalt und Nationalitätenproblem," 53; *Europa irredenta* . . . , 137

Böhm, Adolf, *Die zionistische Bewegung*, 417

Bohn, A., *Sur la Notion de nationalité* . . . , 14
Bolingbroke, 130, 353
Bonald, Vicomte de, 130
Borochov, B., 413; *Sozialismus und Zionismus* . . . , 430
Borries, K., *Kant als Politiker* . . . , 161; *Die Romantik und die Geschichte* . . . , 174
Boulainvilliers, 258
Bourgin, G., *La Formation de l'unité italienne*, 319
Boutmy, É., *The English People* . . . , 350; *Éléments d'une psychologie politique du peuple américain*, 367
Boutroux, É., 136
Bouvy, É., "De Dante à Alfieri . . . ," 324
Boyajian, Z. C., "Raffi . . . ," 392
Brandt, Otto, *A. W. Schlegel* . . . , 177
Breitling, R., *Paul de Lagarde* . . . , 202
Brinton, C., *The Jacobins* . . . , 267
Brockelmann, K., *Das Nationalgefuhl der Turken* . . . , 389
Broecker, R., "Völkerrecht-Minderheitenrecht-Volksrecht," 52
Brooks, R. C., *Civic Training in Switzerland* . . . , 316
Brown, S. M., "Mazzini and Dante," 328
Brun, C., *Le Régionalisme*, 286; *Mistral*, 292
Brunhes, J., *La Géographie de l'histoire*, 32; *Geographie humaine de la France*, 257
Brunot, F., *Histoire de la langue française* . . . , 261
Bryce, James, "The Principle of Nationality . . . ," 141
Buber, M., 416; *Die Judische Bewegung*, 425; 426
Bubnoff, N. von, "Der Begriff der Nation . . . ,"56
Buck, C. D., "Language and the Sentiment of Nationality," 80
Buell, R. L., *International Relations*, 3
Bulle, O., *Die italienische Einheitsidee* . . . ,324
Bülow, Prince von, 151
Bülow, Dietrich von, 151
Bülow, Joachim von, 151
Bunsen, C. K. J. von, 192
Burckhardt, J., 152
Bureau, P., 77
Burke, Edmund, 130, 353

Campbell, Olive Dame, *The Danish Folk School* . . . , 312
Cantalupo, R., "Enrico Corradini and Italian Nationalism," 321
Cappis, O. B., *Die Idee des Kleinstaates* . . . , 152
Carducci, G., 325
Carlyle, Thomas, 357
Cavour, 320a, 333, 334, 335
Cecil, Lord Hugh, Richard Heathcote, *Nationalism and Catholicism*, 76
Chaadayev, P., 241
Chamberlain, H. S., 151, 204
Chandra Pal, 404
Charles Albert of Sardinia, 320, 330
Chateaubriand, 270, 281
Chenu, C., *La Ligue des patriotès*, 283
Chevalier, J., 77

Chirol, V., *The Egyptian Problem*, 385
Chitambar, J. R., *Mahatma Gandhi* . . . , 403
Chuquet, A., *Les Chants patriotiques de l'Allemagne, 1813–1918*, 189
Cihlar, S., "Der Zusammenbruch des Jugoslavismus," 52
Civijic, J., "Studies in Jugoslav Psychology," 252
Clarke, Fred, 112
Clarkson, J. D., *Labour and Nationalism in Ireland*, 360
Class, H., 151
Cleinow, G., ". . . Nationalitätenpolitik in der Sowjetunion," 244
Clough, S. B., *A History of the Flemish Movement* . . . , 300
Cobban, A., *Rousseau and the Modern State*, 264a; *Edmund Burke* . . . , 353
Codignola, E., 112
Cohen, Hermann, *Jüdische Schriften*, 425
Coleridge, S. T., 353, 354
Collins, Michael, 363
Comte, Auguste, 130
Condorcet, 265
Constant, Benjamin, 281
Corradini, E., 321
Culbertson, W. S., "Raw Materials and Foodstuffs in the Commercial Policies of Nations," 103
Cunow, H., *Marxche . . . Staatstheorie*, 108
Cuoco, V., 323
Curtius, E. R., *Maurice Barrès* . . . , 278

Dadabhoy Naoroji, 404
Danilevski, N., 243
Dante, 138, 324, 325, 328
Das, C. R., 409
Daumont, F., *Le Mouvement flamand*, 302
Davitt, M., 362
Dayanandi Saraswati, 404
Deak, F., 225, 226
Dehn, Paul, 151
De Jonge, A. R., *Gottfried Kinkel* . . . , 193
Delaisi, F., *Political Myths and Economic Realities*, 94
Delle-Donne, O., *European Tariff Policies since the War*, 104
Denis, Ernest, *La Bohème depuis la Montagne-Blanche*, 228; *La Question d' Autriche* . . . , 235
Dernburg, B., 151
Déroulède, P., 283, 284, 285
Desjardins, P., See Stewart, H. F., 272
Destrée, J., *Wallons et Flamands* . . . , 304
Dilke, C. W., 357
Dilthey, W., "Schleiermachers politische Gesinnung . . . ," 180
Dittmann, F., *Der Begriff des Volksgeistes bei Hegel*, 163
Dix, A., 151
Dobranitzki, M., "Die Nationalitätenpolitik der Sowjet-Union," 244
Dominian, L., *The Frontiers of Language and Nationality* . . . ," 79
Dorosenko, D., "Die Entwicklung der ukrainischen Geschichtsidee . . . ," 241
Drachsler, J., *Democracy and Assimilation*, 370
Driesmanns, H,. 49, 151

Drinkwater, J., *Patriotism in Literature*, 349
Droysen, J. G., 152, 195, 196, 197
Drüner, H., "Der nationale und der universale Gedanke bei dem Freiherrn vom Stein," 185
Dubnow, S. M., 413; *Die Grundlagen des Nationaljudentums*, 431
Dubos, J. B., 258
Dubreuil, L., *L'Idée regionaliste sous la Révolution*, 289
Ducray, C., *Paul Déroulède, 1846-1914*, 284
Duhamel, M., *La Question bretonne* . . . , 298
Duhring, E., 199
Dumur, L., *Les deux Suisse, 1914-1917*, 314
Dunning, W. A., *A History of Political Theories* . . . , 135
Durkheim, E., 279
Dutt, R. P., *Modern India*, 406
Dwelshauvers, G., *La Catalogne* . . . , 346
Dyboski, R., "Literature and National Life in Modern Poland," 237

Eberz, D., "Die gallikanische Kirche als Werkzeug der Revanche," 274
Eckardt, J. von, 151
Eddy, G. S., *Challenge of the East*, 381
Einstein, Lewis, *Tudor Ideals*, 352
Eisenmann, L., "Quelques Aspects nouveaux de l'idée de nationalité," 56
Elviken, A., *Die Entwicklung des norwegischen Nationalismus*, 307
Emery, J. A., 270
Emin, A., *Development of Modern Turkey*, 390
Engelbrecht, H. C., *J. G. Fichte* . . . , 164
Engeln, O. D., *Inheriting the Earth*, 71
Engels, F., 108
Ergang, R. R., *Herder* . . . , 158
Erler, G. H. J., *Das Recht der nationalen Minderheiten*, 120
Ernst, R., "Der Autonomiegedanke in Elsass-Lothringen," 54

Fairchild, H. N., *The Romantic Quest*. 354
Fairchild, H. P., *The Melting-Pot Mistake*, 369
Falnes, O. J., *National Romanticism in Norway*, 308
Febvre, L. "Langue et nationalité en France," 261
Feder, G., *Der deutsche Staat* . . . , 214
Feldmann, W., *Geschichte der politischen Ideen im Polen*, 237
Fels, J., *Begriff und Wesen der Nation*, 10
Fénelon, 258
Fenske, W., *J. G. Droysen* . . . , 195
Ferry, Jules, 276
Fichte, J. G., 130, 138, 139, 145, 151, 153, 160, 164. 165, 166, 167, 172, 187, 264
Finot, J., *Race Prejudice*, 70
Fircks. W.. "Minderheitenautonomie in Lettland," 54
Fischel, A., *Der Panslawismus* . . . , 227; *Das tschechische Volk*, 230
Fischer, Aloys, 112
Foscolo, Ugo, 322, 323
Fouillée. A., *Esquisse psychologique* . . . , 63; 70

Foulon, F., *La Question wallone*, 305
Fournol, E., *Les Nations romantiques*, 138
Francke, A. H., 144
Francke, Kuno, *Weltbürgerthum in der deutschen Literatur* . . . , 154
Frank, Walter, *Nationalismus und Demokratie im Frankreich* . . . , 275
Frantz, Constantin, 9, 151, 152
Franz, G., *Bismarcks Nationalgefuhl*, 200
Frederick the Great, 187
Fréret, N., 258
Friedlander, I., "Dubnow's Theory of Jewish Nationalism." 430
Froude, J. A., 357
Furniss, S., *The Position of the Laborer in a System of Nationalism*, 100

Gai, L., 253
Galitzi, C., *Assimilation among the Roumanians* . . . , 372
Gandhi, M., 403, 404
Ganivet, A., 346
Gardner, E. G., *The National Idea in Italian Literature*, 325
Gardner, M. M., *Adam Mickiewicz*, 238; *Kosciuszko*, 239
Garibaldi, 332
Garner, J. W., *Political Science and Government*, 2
Gasparian, A., *Begriff der Nation in der deutschen Geschichtsschreibung* . . . , 197
Gaulis, B. G., *Le Nationalisme égyptien*, 386; *La Question arabe*, 391
Gaus, J. M., *Great Britain* . . . , 351
Gazley, J. G., *American Opinion of German Unification*, 201
Gedicke, F., 157
Geist-Lanyi, P., *Das Nationalitätenproblem auf dem Reichstag zu Kremsier*, 220
Gerlach, E. L. von, 156
Gershoy, L., "Barère . . . ," 267
Gervinus, G. G., 152
Gewehr, W. M., *Rise of Nationalism in the Balkans*, 249
Geyl. P., "Einheit und Entzweiung in den Niederlanden," 306
Ghose, 404
Gibbons, H. A., *Nationalism and Internationalism*, 133
Gilbert, F., *J. G. Droysen* . . . , 196
Gill, C., *National Power and Prosperity*, 102
Ginsberg, Asher, 410, 416; *Ten Essays on Zionism*, 424
Ginsburg, I., 207
Gioberti, V., 138, 320, 325, 327
Gneisenau, 145
Gneist, R., 9
Gobineau, Arthur de, 204. 258
Goeken, W., *Herder als Deutscher*, 159
Goerres, J., 151, 183
Goethe, 153
Gokhale. 404
Gooch, G. P., *Nationalism*, 131; *Germany and the French Revolution*, 168
Gooch, R. K., *Regionalism in France*, 291
Gordon, A. D., 416
Goyau, G., 77
Greenfield, K. R., *Economics and Liberalism in the Risorgimento*, 320a
Gregoire, Abbe, 270

Gregory of Tours, 258
Grentrup, T., *Religion und Muttersprache*, 75
Grommaire, G., *La Littérature patriotique en Allemagne*, 188
Grosjean, G., *Le Sentiment national dans la Guerre de Cent Ans*, 262
Grosse, F., "Belgische Nationalitätenfrage," 299
Grousset, R., *Le Reveil de l'Asie*, 380
Gruber, H., "Nationalismus in der französischen Fremaurerei," 27
Gruntvig, Bishop, 311, 312
Guérard, A. L., "Maurice Barrès . . . ," 278
Gurian, W., *Integrale Nationalismus in Frankreich*, 279
Guy-Grand, G., *La Philosophie nationaliste*, 282
Gwynn, D. R., *Edward Martyn* . . . , 364

Haas, Albert, "Der pan-hispanische Gedanke in Amerika," 346
Haas, Jacob de, *Theodor Herzl*, 423
Hacker, L. M., 376
Hackett, F., *Ireland* . . . , 359
Halecki, O., 77
Halévy, Elie, 51
Haller, K. L. von, 145, 152
Hamann, J. G., 144
Hamélius, P., *Histoire politique et littéraire du mouvement flamand*, 301
Hancock, W. K., *Ricascoli* . . . , 331
Handelsmann, M., "Le Rôle de la nationalité dans l'histoire du moygen age," 128
Handman, M., "The Sentiment of Nationalism," 56
Hankins, F. H., *Racial Basis of Civilization*, 68
Hanly, J., *The National Ideal* . . . , 354
Hapgood, N., *Professional Patriots*, 373
Harden, M., 151
Hardenberg, Prince von, 145
Hardie, J. Keir, "Michael Davitt," 362
Harper, S. N., *Civic Training in Soviet Russia*, 246
Harris, Hugh, "Greek Origins of the Idea of Cosmopolitanism," 124
Hartmann, L. M., "Die Nation als politischer Faktor," 49
Hasse, Ernst, 151
Hasselblatt, W., 52, 54
Hassinger, H., *Entwicklung des tschechischen Nationalbewusstseins*, 229
Haupt, H., *Quellen* . . . *zur Geschichte der Burschenschaft*, 190
Hauser, Henri, *Le Principe des nationalités*, 136; *Probléme du regionalisme*, 296
Haushofer, K., *Geopolitik der Pan-Ideen*, 89
Havlicek, K., 228
Hay, Joseph, *Staat, Volk und Weltbürgertum* . . . , 157
Hayes, Carlton J. H., *Essays on Nationalism*, 1; "Two Varieties of Nationalism," 1; *Historical Evolution of Modern Nationalism*, 130; "Contributions of Herder to the Doctrine of Nationalism," 158; *France, a Nation of Patriots*, 277; "Bolingbroke," 353

Haymann, F., *Weltburgertum und Vaterlandsliebe* . . . , 264
Hazard, P., *La Révolution française et les lettres italiennes*, 323
Hecker, J. F., *Russian Sociology*, 242
Heer, G., 190
Hegel, 9, 139, 145, 151, 160, 162, 163, 195
Heiden, K., *Geschichte des National Sozialismus*, 211
Heissenbutel, K. H. T., *Volk und Nation* . . . , 127
Heller, H., *Sozialismus und Nation*, 109; *Politische Ideenkreise*, 139; *Hegel*, 162; *Europa und der Fascismus*, 339
Hennessy, J., *Régions de France*, 293
Herben, J., "Karl Havlicek," 228
Herbert, S., *Nationality and Its Problems*, 28
Herder, J. G., 130, 138, 154, 158, 159, 163, 227, 310, 329
Herrnritt, R., *Nationalitat und Recht*, 222
Hertz, F., "Allgemeine Theorien vom Nationalcharakter," 25; "Wesen und Werden der Nation," 50; *Race and Civilization*, 67; "Englischer Nationalismus," 347
Herzl, Theodor, 416, 423
Hess, Moses, 416, 422
Hettick, E. L., *A Study in Ancient Nationalism*, 126
Heuss, T., *Hitler's Weg*, 212
Hevesy, A., *Nationalities in Hungary*, 226
Heyking, A., *La Conception de l'État* . . . , 93
Hildebrand, G., 151
Hintze, H., "Der französische Regionalismus," 53; "Der französische Regionalismus und seine Wurzeln," 286; *Staatseinheit und Foderalismus*, 287
Hintze, Otto, 185
Hitler, A., 207a
Hobson, J. A., *Psychology of Jingoism*, 61; *Imperialism*, 98
Hoffmann-Linke, E., *Nationalismus und Demokatie* . . . , 265
Holcombe, A. N., *Chinese Revolution*, 395
Holdheim, G., *Theoretische Grundlagen des Zionismus*, 418
Homyakov, A., 241
Hoover, Calvin B., *Germany Enters the Third Reich*, 210
Hormayr, Baron de, 191a
Horten, M., "Muhammed Abduh," 288
Hotman, F., 258
Hugelmann, K., "Anschlussbewegung," 54; "Mittelalterliches und modernes Nationalitätenproblem, 128; Deutsche Nation . . . im Mittelalter," 143
Huizinga, J., *Wege der Kulturgeschichte*, 306
Humboldt, Wilhelm von, 145
Humphrey, E. F., *Nationalism and Religion in America*, 368
Hunter, E. L., *Sociological Analysis of Patriotism*, 38
Hyslop, B. F., *French Nationalism in 1789* . . . , 266

Isocrates, 125
Israel, A., *L'École de la république* . . . , 276
Ivanov, Y., "Le Peuple bulgare," 248
Izard, G., See Mounier, E., 285a

Jahn, L., 151, 186
Jakabssy, E., "Ungarische Minoritäten," 54
Jamal al-Din al-Afghani, 388
Janowsky, O. I., *Jews and Minority Rights*, 413
Jastrow, I., *Geschichte des deutschen Einheitstraumes*, 142
Jaszi, O., *Dissolution of the Habsburg Monarchy*, 218
Jaucourt, 263
Jean-Desthieux, F., *Evolution régionaliste*, 294; *Produire*, 295
Jerusalem, Franz, *Begriff der Nation*, 11
Jeschke, H., "Angel Ganivet," 346
Joachimsen, P., *Vom deutschen Volk zum deutschen Staat*, 143
Joan of Arc, 262
Johannet, R., *Le Principe des nationalités*, 4; 51, 77
Joseph, Bernard, *Nationality*, 8
Junghann, O., *National Minorities*, 118; See also Boehm, M. H., 52
Jüthner, J., *Hellenen und Barbaren*, 125

Kallen, H. M., *Culture and Democracy* . . . , 371
Kallenbach, J., "Adam Mickiewicz," 238
Kandel, I. L., *Educational Yearbook* . . . , 112
Kant, 160, 161, 163, 204
Kármán, E. von, "Psychologie der Internationalismus," 50
Katsch, H., *Heinrich von Treitschke* . . . , 198
Kautsky, K., "Nationalität und Internationalität," 107, 108; *Are the Jews a Race?*, 414
Kawerau, S., *Denkschrift* . . . , 208
Kayser, E. L., *Jeremy Bentham* . . . , 356
Keats, J., 354
Keith, A., *Nationality and Race*, 72
Keshab Chandra Sen, 404
Kettle, T. M., "Michael Davitt," 362
Keyser, R. J., 307
King, Bolton, *History of Italian Unity*, 310; *Mazzini*, 328
Kinkel, G., 193
Kirchhoff, A., *Die Begriffe Nation und Nationalität*, 12
Kireyevsky, I. V., 241
Kjellén, R., *Staat als Lebensform*, 88
Klamroth, K., *Paul de Lagarde*, 203
Klatzkin, J., *Probleme des modernen Judentums*, 412
Klausner, J., *History of Modern Hebrew Literature*, 428
Kleist, H. von, 171
Kluckhohn, P., *Persönlichkeit und Gemeinschaft*, 171
Kohn, Hans, *Nationalism in the Soviet Union*, 244; *History of Nationalism in the East*, 378; *Die Europäisierung des Orients*, 379; *Nationalism and Imperialism in the Hither East*, 382; *Nationalismus* . . . , 410; *L'Humanisme juif*, 416; *Martin Buber* . . . , 426
Koht, H., "L'Ésprit national . . ." 137; *Les Luttes des paysans*, 307, 309
Kollar, J., 231
Kosciuszko, T., 239
Kosok, P., *Modern Germany*, 207

Koyré, A., *La Philosophie et le problème national en Russie* . . . , 241
Kranel, R., 151
Krehbiel, E. B., *Nationalism, War and Society*, 41
Krek, J., 253
Krizanic, J., 241
Kronenberg, M., *Der politische Gedanke*, 34
Kruscewski, W., "Der französische Nationsbegriff," 263
Kühn, J., *Der Nationalismus in Leben der dritten Republik*, 274
Kuhne, W., "Entwicklung des polnischen Nationalgefühls," 237
Kurth, G., *La Nationalité belge*, 299

Lagarde, Paul de, 151, 202, 203
Lajpat Rai, 404; *Young India*, 407
Lalic, N., "Les Idées de Strossmayer," 253
Lamprecht, K., 151, 197
Langbehn, J., 151
Lange, F., 151
Langsam, W., *The Napoleonic Wars and German Nationalism in Austria*, 191
Lanz, H., "The Philosophy of Kirievsky," 241
Laski, H. J., *Grammar of Politics*, 90; *Nationalism and the Future of Civilization*, 91
La Tour du Pin, 281
Laum, B., *Die geschlossene Wirtschaft*, 215
Laurian, M. A., *Le Principe des Nationalités*, 254
Lavater, J. K., 144
Le Bon, G., *The Psychology of Peoples*, 62
Lednicki, W., "Poland and the Slavophil Idea," 237
Leemans, V., "Soziologie des flämischen Nationalismus," 301
Le Fur, L., *Races, Nationalités, États*, 30; 77
Leibnitz, 160
Lemberg, E., *Grundlagen des nationalen Erwachens in Böhmen*, 232
Lenin, N., *Über die nationale Frage*, 110; 244
Lenz, M., "Nationalität und Religion," 74; "Deutsche Nationalempfinden im Zeitalter unserer Klassiker," 154
Léon, X., *Fichte*, 166
Leontiev, K., 243
Lieber, Francis, *On Nationalism and Internationalism*, 84
List, F., 130, 151, 199
Locher, P. J. G., *National Differenzierung* . . . *der Slowaken und Tschechen*, 236
Loesch, K. C., *Volk unter Völkern*, 53; *Staat und Volkstum*, 54
Loiseau, C., "La Politique de Strossmayer," 253
Louis XVI, 263
Luden, H., 231
Lund, H., See Begtrup, H., 311
Luzio, A., 335

Mably, 258
Macartney, C. A., *National States and National Minorities*, 117a
MacCallum, E., *Nationalist Crusade in Syria*, 392

McDougall, W., *Group Mind*, 64; Ethics and *Some Modern World Problems*, 65
Machiavelli, 138, 325
Madariaga, S. de, *Englishmen, Frenchmen, Spaniards*, 66; *Spain*, 338
Mair, E., *Psychologie der nationalen Minderheit*, 121
Maistre, J. De, 270, 271
Manniche, P., See Begtrup, H., 311
Manzoni, A., 324
Margulies, H., *Kritik der Zionismus*, 421
Markovic, S., 253
Marraro, H. R., *American Opinion on Unification of Italy*, 336; *Nationalism in Italian Education*, 344
Marriott, J. A. R., *Makers of Modern Italy*, 321
Martin-Saint-Léon, E., *Sociétés de la Nation* . . . , 260
Martyn, E., 364
Marx, Karl, 108
Massaryk, T. G., *Spirit of Russia*, 240
Mathiez, A., *Origines des cultes revolutionnaires*, 269
Matl. J., "Entstehung des jugoslawischen Staates," 252
Matter, P., *Cavour* . . . , 334
Maurras, C., 130, 273, 275, 279, 280, 281
Maury, J. S., 270
Mausbach, J., "Nationalismus und christlicher Universalismus," 78
Mauss, M., 51
Mazzini, G., 130, 138, 158, 320, 325, 328, 329
Megaro G., *Alfieri*, 326
Meinecke, F., 10; *Weltbürgertum und Nationalstaat*, 145; 173; 185
Meinert, F., 232
Merriam, C. E., *Making of Citizens*, 87
Metternich, 191, 319
Meyer, F., "Kants Stellung zu Nation und Staat," 161
Mezeray, M., 258
Michels, R., *Der Patriotismus*, 27; "Entwicklung des Vaterlandsgedankens," 49; "Amerikanischer Nationalitäts Begriff," 367
Mickiewicz, A., 238
Miliukov, P., *Mouvement intellectual russe*, 243
Mill, John Stuart, *Representative Government*, 83
Miller, H. A., *Races, Nations and Classes*, 57
Mirabeau, 265
Mirtschuk, L., "Messianismus bei den Slaven," 227
Mises, L., *Nation, Staat und Wirtschaft*, 96
Mistral, 292
Mitscherlich, W., *Nationalismus*, 5; "Volk und Nation," 6; 10; *Nationalstaat und Nationalwirtschaft*, 97
Moeller van den Bruck, A., 137
Mohl, R. von. 159
Molisch, P., *Deutsch-nationale Bewegung in Oesterreich*, 148; *Kampf der Tschechen* . . . , 234
Moltke, Helmuth. 151
Mommsen. T., 152
Montesquieu, 258. 265
Monti, V., 323, 324
Mookerji. R., *Nationalism in Hindu Culture*, 408

Moser, F. C. von, 155
Mounier, E., *Charles Péguy*, 285a
Muhammad Abduh, 388
Muhammad Rashid Rida, 388
Muhl, M., *Antike Menschheitsidee*, 124
Muir, R., *Nationalism and Internationalism*, 37
Müller, Adam, 145, 152, 171, 172, 173
Munch, P. A., 307
Muret, C. T., *French Royalist Doctrine* . . . , 281
Murko, M., *Deutsche Einflüsse* . . . , 231
Murray, Gilbert, 51
Murray, W. S., *Making of the Balkan States*, 250
Musebeck, E., *Schleiermacher* . . . , 180

Nadler, J., "Nation, Staat, Dichtung," 216
Natorp, P. G., *Der Deutsche und sein Staat*, 147
Naumann, F., 151
Niebuhr, B. G., 152
Nietzsche, F., 154, 204, 207a
Nothomb, P., "Enrico Corradini . . . ," 321
Novalis, 144, 145, 171, 172, 176, 310

Oakesmith, J., *Race and Nationality*, 347
Obradovic, D., 253
Omladina, 253
Oncken, H., "Deutsche geistige Einflüsse . . . ," 231
Oppenheimer, Franz, 10; "Rassentheoretische Geschichtsphilosophie," 49
Oudendijk, K. E., "Grossniederländische Bewegung," 54
Owen, D. E., *Imperialism and Nationalism in the Far East*, 394

Page, Kirby, *National Defense*, 40; *Dollars and World Peace*, 101; *Imperialism and Nationalism*, 384
Palacky, F., 231
Parini, G., 324
Pariset, G., *Études* . . . , 290
Partridge, G. E., *Psychology of Nations*, 58
Pasquier, E., 258
Pasvolsky, L., *Economic Nationalism of the Danubian States*, 251
Paul-Dubois, L., "Grundtvig 312
Peake, C. H., *Nationalism and Education in Modern China*, 398
Peardon, T. P., *Transition in English Historical Writing*, 355
Pearson, Karl, *National Life* . . . , 73
Pécaut, F., 112
Péguy, C., 285a
Péguy, M., See Mounier, E., 285a
Perla, L., *National Honor*, 42
Petrarch, 325
Petrescu, N., *Interpretation of National Differentiations*, 26
Pfitzner, J., "Luden und Palacky," 231
Pierce, Bessie, *Civic Attitudes* . . . , 374; *Citizens' Organizations* . . . , 375
Pillsbury, W. B., *Psychology of Nationality*, 59
Pinon, R.. 77
Pinson, K. S., *Pietism and German Nationalism*. 144
Pius IX, 320
Plato, 125

Platz, H., *Geistige Kämpfe in modernen Frankreich*, 273; "Der Nationalismus im französischen Denken," 274
Pole, D. G., *India in Transition*, 401
Pollard, A. F., *Factors in Modern History*, 134
Pollock, F., 51
Portalis, 270
Powers, G. C., *Nationalism at the Council of Constance*, 129
Prazak, A., "The Slavonic Congress of 1848," 236
Preuss, G. F., *Quellen des Nationalgeistes der Befreiungskriege*, 187
Preuss, W., See Holdheim, G., 418
Prevet, F., *Régionalisme économique*, 297
Pribram, K., "Deutscher Nationalismus und deutscher Sozialismus," 108

Radl, E., *Kampf zwischen Tschechen und Deutschen*, 233
Raffi, 392
Ram Mohan Roy, 404
Ranke, L. von, 9, 145, 197
Rapp, A., *Der deutsche Gedanke*, 149
Raschhofer, H., "Die nationale Kurie . . . ," 52
Ratzel, F., 151
Ray, P. C., *C. R. Das*, 409
Redslob, R., *Principe des nationalités . . . ,*92
Reidenbach, C., *Critical Analysis of Patriotism*, 39
Reidt, K., *Nationale und Übernationale bei Fichte . . . ,* 167
Reimer, J. L., 151
Reinhard, J. "Schleiermacher . . . ," 180
Reisner, E. H., *Nationalism in Education . . . ,*111
Renan, E., *Qu'est-ce qu'une Nation*, 15; 70, 136
Renner, Bruno, *F. K. von Moser . . . ,* 155
Renner, Karl, *Selbstbestimmungsrecht der Nationen*, 105; *Staat und Nation*, 221
Reuter, H., "Schleiermacher . . . ," 180
Reventlow, Count, 151
Ricasoli, B., 331
Ritter, G., *Stein . . . ,* 185
Robert, A., *L'idée nationale autrichienne . . . ,* 191a
Robinson, J., "Altjüdische Autonomie Begriff," 52; *Minoriträten Probleme*, 56
Rocco, A., "Political Doctrine of Fascism," 337
Rochow, F. von, 156
Rodbertus, Karl, 130
Rodes, J., *La Chine nationaliste*, 400
Roffenstein, G., "Zur Soziologie des Nationalismus . . . ," 50
Rohden, P., *De Maistre . . . ,* 271
Rohrbach, P., 151
Rose, J. Holland, *Nationality in Modern History*, 132
Rosenberg, Alfred, *Wesengefüge des Nationsozialismus*, 213; *Mythus des 20. Jahrhunderts*, 216
Rosenbluth, F., *Volk und Nation*, 13
Rothfels, H., 185; "Bismarck . . . ," 200
Rotteck, Karl von, 152
Rousseau, 130, 204, 263, 264, 264a, 265
Roux, M., *Charles Maurras . . . ,* 280

Roy, M. N., *Revolution und Konterrevolution in China*, 399; *Indien*, 405
Royar-Collard, P. P., 281
Ruhlmann, P., "Revanche Gedanke . . . ," 274
Ruppin, A., *Soziologie der Juden*, 411
Ruth, H., *Arndt . . . ,* 184
Ruyssen, T., 51
Ryan, John, 77

Sabry, M., *La Genèse de l'esprit national égyptien*, 387
Sadler, M., 112
Safarik, P., 231
Salm, M., "Angriffsgedanke in der französischen Militärliteratur," 274
Salmon, Lucy, *Newspaper and Authority*, 115
Salomon, G., *Nation und Nationalität*, 50; *Das Mittelalter . . . ,* 175
Salz, A., "Nationalismus und Sozialismus . . . ," 207
Samassa, P., *Völkerstreit im Hapsburgerstaat*, 219
Samuel, Richard, *Novalis . . . ,* 176
Sato, E. M., "Revival of Pure Shinto," 393
Schaeffle, A., 151
Scheler, M., *Nation und Weltanschauung*, 18
Schelling, 171
Schiemann, T., 151
Schlegel, A. W., 170, 177
Schlegel, Friedrich, 130, 145, 151, 152, 170, 171, 172, 178, 179
Schleiermacher, Friedrich, 144, 171, 178, 180, 181, 182
Schlözer, A. L., 227
Schlund, E., *Katholizismus und Vaterland*, 78
Schmahl, E., *Aufstieg der nationalen Idee*, 150
Schmid, F., "Recht der Nationalitäten," 49
Schmidt, H., *F. J. Stahl . . . ,* 197a
Schmidt-Rohr, G., *Die Sprache . . . ,* 81
Schmitt, Carl, *Politische Romantik*, 173
Schnabel, F., *Deutsche Geschichte . . . ,* 146
Schnee, H., *Nationalismus und Imperialismus*, 99
Schneider, Herbert, *Making of the Fascist State*, 337; *Making Fascists*, 342
Schopenhauer, A., 204
Schroth, H., *Welt-und Staatsideen der deutschen Liberalismus*, 194
Scott, J. F., *Menace of Nationalism . . . ,* 113; *Patriots in the Making*, 114
Scott, Walter, 354
Seely, R., 357
Seillière, E., 77, 204
Seipel, I., 10; *Nation und Staat*, 17
Seton-Watson, R. W., *Rise of Nationality in the Balkans*, 248
Sheehy-Skeffington, F., *Michael Davitt . . . ,* 362
Shepardson, W. H., "Nationalism and American Trade," 377
Shmurlo, E., "From Krizanic to the Slavophils," 241
Sieburg, F., *Es Werde Deutschland*, 209; *Who Are These French?*, 256
Siegfried, A., *France*, 255
Sieyès, Abbe, 258, 268
Silone, I., *Der Fascismus*, 343

Simar, T., "La Doctrine des races . . . ," 69

Simon, Leon, Studies in Jewish Nationalism, 420

Snyder, L. L., From Bismarck to Hitler, 207a

Solmi, A., Making of Modern Italy, 322

Soloviev, V., 243

Sommer, A., Friedrich List . . . , 199

Southey, R., 353

Spann, O., Wesen des Volkstums, 24; 172

Spener, P. J., 144

Spiegel, S., Hebrew Reborn, 427

Srbik, H. R. von, 200

Stahl, F., 9, 197a

Stalin, J., 110; Leninism, 110a; 244

Stavenhagen, K., "Kulturnation und Staatsnation," 12; "Muttersprache," 80

Stein, Baron vom, 145, 185

Stein, Leonard, Zionism, 419

Stein, Lorenz, 9

Steinacker, W., Begriff der Volkszugehörigkeit . . . , 224

Steinmetz, S. R., Nationalitaten in Europa, 43; "Die Nationalität und ihr Wille," 50

Stengel, Karl von, 151

Stephens, H. M., "Nationality and History," 132

Stern, A., Einfluss der französischen Revolution . . . , 169

Stewart, H. F., French Patriotism . . . , 272

Stocks, J. L., Patriotism and the Super State, 35

Stoecker, A., 207a

Stojanovic, J. D., "The First Slavophils . . . ," 241

Stratton, G. M., Social Psychology of International Conduct, 60

Strossmayer, J., 253

Sturzo, L., 77; Italy and Fascismo, 338

Sulzbach, W., "Begriff und Wesen der Nation," 56; Nationales Gemeinschaftsgefühl und wirtschaftliches Interesse, 95

Sun Yat Sen, 395, 396, 399

Suranyi-Ungar, T., "Wirtschaft und Nationalismus . . . ," 399

Sybel, H. von, 197

Syed Ahmad Khan, 404

Tagore, R., Nationalism, 19; 404

Taine, H., 70, 130, 273

T'ang Leang-li, China in Revolt, 396; Foundations of Modern China, 397

Tartakower, A., "Geschichte des jüdichen Sozialismus," 430

Techet, C., Völker, Vaterländer und Fursten, 45

Tharaud, J., Déroulède . . . , 285

Thayer, W. R., Dawn of Italian Independence, 318; Cavour, 333

Tiander, K., Erwachen Osteuropas . . . , 241a

Tieck, L., 310

Tilak, 404

Tobien, A., Livländische Ritterschaft . . . , 247

Tonnesen, J., "Volkstum und nationale Gedanke," 54

Tönnies, F., 49

Topa, I. N., National Thought in India, 402

Townsend, M. E., Modern German Colonialism . . . , 205

Trampler, K., Staaten und nationale Gemeinschaften, 122; Krise des Nationalstaats, 123

Treitschke, H. von, 9, 151, 152, 197, 198, 207a

Trevelyan, G. M., Garibaldi 332

Trotsky, L., "Nationalism and Economic Life," 95

Turgot, 263

Turner, F. J., Sections in American History, 376

Uhlmann, J., Görres . . . , 183

Ulbricht, W., Bunsen . . . , 192

Ullmann, H., "Anschlussbewegung . . . ," 54

Unger, F., Schrifttum des Nationalsozialismus, 216a

Ungern-Sternberg, A. von, Schleiermacher . . . , 182

Unold, J., 151

Vallaux, C., See Brunhes, J., 32

Vallis, M., "Enrico Corradini . . . ." 321

Vandervelde, E., "Belgian Foreign Policy . . . ," 304

Van Deusen, G., Sieyès . . . , 268

Van Gennep, A., Traité comparatif des nationalités, 29; Le nationalité géorgienne, 392

Vattier, G., Mentalité canadienne-française, 366

Vaussard, M., Enquête . . . , 75

Veblen, T., Nature of Peace 36

Verschoor, A. D., Ältere deutsche Romantik. 170

Vidal, C., Charles-Albert . . . , 330

Vierkandt. A., 10

Vinacke, H. M., History of the Far East, 393

Vincenty, C., Nationalités en Hongrie, 225

Vivekananda. 404

Volpers, R., F. Schlegel . . . , 178

Voltaire. 263, 265

Vosberg-Rekow, M., 151

Vossler, Karl. Language and the Spirit of Civilization, 80

Vossler, Otto, Mazzini . . . , 329

Vries, A. de. "Nationalitätenpolitik Sowjetenrusslands," 53

Wagner, K., 151

Wagner. Richard, 204, 207a

Walek-Czernecki. T., "Nationalité dans l'antiquité." 126

Wallace. W. S., Canadian Nationalism. 365

Wallach. R., Abendländische Gemeinschaftsbewusstsein . . . , 128

Wallner. N., Fichte, 165

Walsh, H. H., Concordat of 1801 . . . , 270

Weber, Alfred, 49

Weber, Max, 49

Wechssler, E., Esprit und Geist, 140

Weilenmann, H., Vielsprachige Schweiz, 315

Weinreich, E., Nation als Lebensgemeinschaft, 46

Welcker, F.. 130, 152

Welhaven, S. C., 307

Wendel, H. J., *Kampf der Südslawen . . .*, 252; *Sudslawischen Risorgimento*, 253
Wentzcke, P., *Quellen . . . zur Geschichte der Burschenschaft*, 190
Wergeland, H., 307
Werner, B. von, 151
Wertheimer, M. S., *Pan-German League*, 206
Whyte, A. J., *Cavour . . .*, 335
Wieneke, E., *Friedrich Schlegel . . .*, 179
William II, 151, 204, 207a
Windelband, W., 274
Wingfield-Stratford, E., *History of British Patriotism*, 348
Winkler, W., *Handbuch der Nationalitäten*, 117
Wirth, A., 151
Wohltmann, F., 151
Woltmann, L., 151
Wolzendorff, K., *Grundgedanken des Rechts der nationalen Minderheiten*, 119
Wordsworth, W., 353, 354

Wuorinen, J. H., *Nationalism in Modern Finland*, 313

Yarmolinsky, A., *Jews and Other Minorities . . .*, 245
Yoshida, Kumaji, 112
Young, George, *Nationalism and War in the Near East*, 383

Zangwill, I., *Principle of Nationalities*, 20
Zbinden, J., *Gioberti . . .*, 327
Zeydel, E. H., *Holy Roman Empire . . .*, 153
Zhitlovsky, C., 413
Zia Goek Alp, 389
Ziegfield, A. H., *See* Loesch, K. C. von, 53
Ziegler, H., *Moderne Nation*, 9
Ziehen, E., "Canadianism," 365
Zimmermann, A., 151
Zimmern, A., *Nationality and Government*, 33
Zinzendorf, 144
Zlocisti, T., *Moses Hess . . .*, 422